WALKS
with WHEELS

CORNWALL

CONTENTS

INTRODUCTION

FRIENDS HAVE PERPETUALLY ASKED FOR WALK RECOMMENDATIONS. THEY KNOW I HAVE HAD YEARS OF EXPERIENCE TAKING BOTH MY DAUGHTERS WHEN YOUNG, MY GRANDMOTHER AND NOW MOTHER OUT AND ABOUT AROUND CORNWALL TO PLACES THAT ARE EASILY ACCESSIBLE (IN THE BROADEST SENSE INCLUDING COST), HAVE REST FACILITIES, INCLUDING TEA/COFFEE, CAKE AND MAYBE A SANDWICH. GENERALLY, I LOVE PLANNING THE DAY OUT AND IF A WALK CAN CATER FOR THOSE DEPENDENT ON WHEELS THEN ALL WILL HAVE THE OPPORTUNITY OF PLEASURE, NO MATTER THEIR AGE AND THEIR LEVEL OF MOBILITY.

My background as a geography lecturer meant that I had to plan and prepare students for fieldtrips, both in the UK and abroad. The first field visit I ever organised was to Kenya, based at a camp with no electricity or running water; dinner walked into the kitchen and we tapped our shoes out every morning for scorpions. We all loved it and got there and back again without incident. Overseeing and accompanying students in the field, observing, taking measurements and ultimately helping them understand the landscape gave me the skills and confidence to organise successful trips for others.

Of course, in the age of well-being and a daily dose of nature, these walks are ideal for staying mentally and physically healthy. Age Concern - www.ageuk.org.uk/information-advice/health-wellbeing gives advice and reasons for the elderly getting outdoors on a regular basis. In particular, I think that the social element

to walking is underestimated and loneliness is increasingly recognised as an issue. Walks with Wheels helps to be social too so it's a win-win situation all round!

The majority of walks I have selected can be wheeled by all types; wheelchairs, electric wheels, children's scooters and buggies. Coincidently, bikes can use most of them too although that is not the focus of this guide and I would refer you to 'Cycling Cornwall' by Tony Farnell for a more appropriately distanced cycling focus. Distances of walks are given rather than times, as this factor will vary so much that the timing seems pointless. This was a purposeful decision as I felt that the variability would be so great depending on the types of and number of wheels. A good walking rate with no wheels of 4.8km/3 miles an hour can give you an idea, but this would be on the flat and without pauses. Having arthritis, I would not be able to achieve this pace, but those I have seen with shoppers pelt along with parents out for a run with an all-terrain three-wheel pushchair.

I hope that by sharing some of my favourite Cornish accessible landscapes you will be inspired to get out and about with your wheels.

Happy wheeling!

Sarah Thomson

HEALTH AND SAFETY

Care and common sense always need to be put into practice when outdoors and especially when responsible for those on wheels. Whether young or old, if sitting for a period of time and outdoors it is very easy for that person to get cold, sunburnt or dehydrated via heat and wind, so be prepared!

WEATHER

It is really important to check the weather before going out. Always have quality high factor sun cream, some water, snacks and an extra blanket with weather appropriate clothing for the wheel user. Both the elderly and young have thinner skin that is prone to burning easily and that can include wind burn too so a classic floppy hat is ideal, one that shades the face and covers those burnable ears.

Unless you have the all-terrain wheelchairs and buggies with big wheels, you carry suitable waterproof coverings or you don't mind getting wet, I would avoid potentially wet and very windy weather. Although some walks are more sheltered than others.

There are multiple places to check weather forecasts including the Met Office.
www.metoffice.gov.uk

TIDES

Buy your own annual local tide timetable booklet! For around £1.50 it is a sound investment. It is always a shame when you see on the local news people who have been isolated by the tide and then need rescuing at an effectively huge expense. Tide times usually contain other information about coastal and beach safety as well as how the tides work.

TOILETS

Toilet facilities in Cornwall vary considerably and I have become a bit of an expert. The majority of public toilets are operated by parish/town council. Sadly, disabled toilets are prone to antisocial behaviour and some use the RADAR key system to help reduce the issue and keep the toilets available to those with mobility problems. RADAR keys are a national system and it is well worth investing in a key, they are not expensive, a few pounds, and available from their website www.radarkeys.org or outlets such as Truro Information Centre in Truro.

Toilets in some places do charge. I have tried to give up-to-date toilet information in the book, as there is nothing worse than finding facilities locked, or caught short for the sake of a coin.

PUBLIC TRANSPORT

Although the car is currently the most dominant form of transport, I have included, and I would actively encourage, the use of public transport wherever possible.

DOGS

Many of us have dogs, including those with mobility issues. The walks are on the whole dog friendly as long as the dog is kept on a lead and suitably cleaned up after when out and about. Some of the walks are by water that has steep banks and a dog would have difficulty getting out if they have been distracted and fallen in. Loose dogs can also scare others, chase wildlife, get in the way of cyclists and generally cause havoc, so please be a responsible dog owner. If adding a beach visit with any of the walks, it may be useful to refer to current Cornwall Council guidelines.

MAPS

All maps referred to in the text are Ordance Survey (OS) Explorer.

01

Japanese Garden

WALK 01

NEWQUAY – ST MAWGAN

OF ALL THE WALKS IN CORNWALL, THIS GIVES A MULTI-SENSORY DELIGHT ALL YEAR ROUND; EACH SEASON HAS SOMETHING DIFFERENT TO OFFER, EVERYONE OF ALL AGES WILL LOVE IT! IT IS A WALKING WITH WHEELS NATURE EXPERIENCE, WHERE THE MATURE WOODLAND ENVELOPS THOSE RAMBLING WITH A TRULY RELAXING WANDER ALONG A PUBLIC FOOTPATH IN PART OF THE CARNANTON ESTATE.

DISTANCE: Easy ramble for those with buggies approximately 3.3km/2miles.

PARKING: SAT NAV TR8 4EP for the post office, the car park is to the rear. OS 106 Explorer Newquay and Padstow 1:25000 with grid reference 873658.

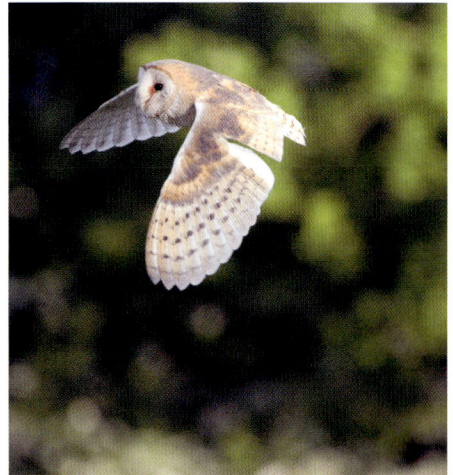

Barn Owls can be seen at dusk

Japanese Garden

- THE WALK -

The walk is on a compressed hard-core path (though this can be muddy so is not necessarily for the buggy proud when wet/ winter). Suitable for dogs on leads – dog poo bin at the start – don't forget bags. This is pheasant country so beware if you have a dog that likes chasing them.

Access St Mawgan village via the B3276, turning right down into the village if coming from the east and before Newquay Airport. If coming from the west and the coast, then turn left again before the Airport and drive down the hill.

The free private car park (hard-core based) is behind the village post office/shop/tearoom just to the left of the Falcon Inn at the bottom of the hill. Times to avoid are when the adjacent primary school has pick-up-time from about 3pm for an hour during term-time. If you have parked here at this time I would wait and go and get an ice cream in the local post office and all the school cars will just evaporate.

To access the public footpath, there is a wooden post indicating the start by the house in the car park, behind the village post office/shop/tearoom. The only spot of difficulty is negotiating the kissing gate beside the house so best to carry the infant past this, have the buggy collapsed and then pop it up on the other side. Don't forget the opportunity for a quick kiss though when passing through.

After passing through the gate, you turn left along the tarmac (this becomes a compressed hard-core path) and simply walk your wheels as far as you wish to go. Just before Lawrey's Mill there is a footbridge and the footpath narrows, after which head up the hill to Higher Tolcarne Farm and the back lane between St Columb Major and Mawgan Porth. The path does undulate and can be a little muddy but the trees, the sound of the river and the wildlife opportunities surely out-weigh a little mud; just be prepared with some boots/wellies if wet!

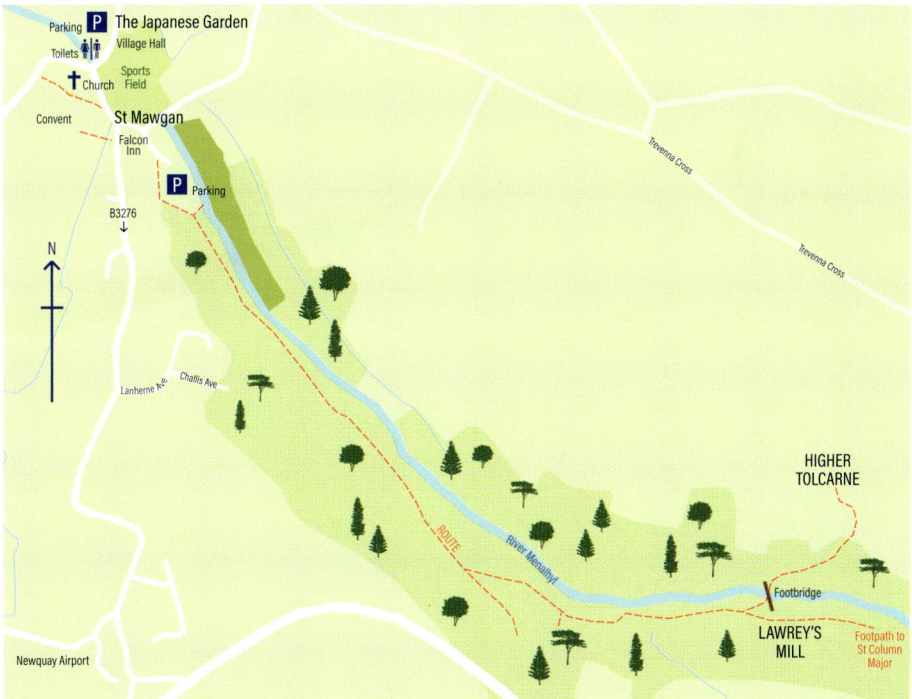

At Lawrey's Mill bear to the left of the wooden footbridge for the perfect opportunity for a game of 'Pooh sticks' and if in the summer, dragonfly spotting. It is then time to turn around and wander back along the path you've come by, providing a totally different vista the other way so that it's almost like a round trip.

- WALK EXTENSION -

When the children are older and you are buggy-less, take the right-hand path before Lawrey's Mill and it will lead you on up the valley to St Columb Major (a further 4km) and the many facilities that this small ex-market town has to offer.

other information

TOILETS: Free in the village just over the bridge towards the Japanese Garden - including disabled - open all year round.

BUSES: 408 Summercourt via Newquay, Porth, Tregurrian, Mawgan Porth, St Mawgan and the Airport A5 Newquay, Porth, Tregurrian, St Mawgan, Mawgan Porth, Porth Cothan, Constantine Bay, Padstow.

DOGS: Are allowed if on leads due to pheasants and river. A large sports field/ village green/cricket field is adjacent to the river with a picket-fenced play area and picnic benches.

FREE PARKING: There is free parking available.

OTHER: There is an annual Feast Day Sports event and Cornish Wrestling in July.

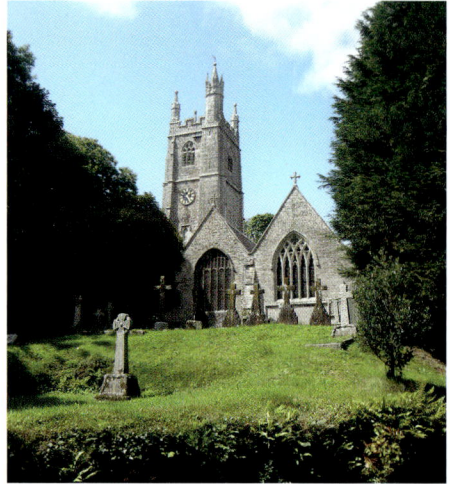

St Mawgan-in-Pydar Church ©Russell Perry

what's nearby

Village 13th Century Church - this is unlocked during the day and has wheelchair access. This beautiful church provides a peaceful place to pause and reflect. There are many historical features both inside and outside the church, including a fine collection of Arundell 16th century brasses, a 1553 carved pulpit, 16th century ornate pew ends and a 15th century stone font. www.lannpydar.org.uk/stmawgan

The Convent/Monastery adjacent to the Church - you can walk the Stations of the Cross along the flat lane to the rear of the original Lanherne Manor but there is a brief, steep climb to access the lane along the very quiet road so a wheelchair may struggle. Note the skull and crossbones carved into the apex of a gateway in the wall to the graveyard where there are Commonwealth War Graves. For times of mass visit www.friendsoflanherne.org

The Japanese Garden
www.japanesegarden.co.uk

—NATURE—

The valley seems to have its own microclimate offering protection from wind. It's warmer in winter and cooler in summer. Actually, this area is designated as an 'Area of Great Landscape Value' and a 'County Wildlife Site'. Designations were created by Cornwall Council because of the quality of the scenery and wildlife, hence the restriction of development.

January has carpets of snow drops by the river and the bare mature ash trees blowing in the wind make magical 'clacking' sounds. Ferns abound and the stone walled bank on the right, as you set off, is positively dripping in various moss and lichen species indicating a clean air environment.

Later in spring, there are swathes of bluebells and ransoms, and summer offers blackberry picking and a chance to see demoiselle dragonflies dancing over the river in dappled sunlight.

Pheasants (I have also seen all black and all white) are plentiful, making a racket when disturbed into a flapping shallow flight. The sound of greater spotted woodpeckers drilling into tree bark for insects can occur. Barn owls hunting may sometimes be observed at dusk in fields near the village.

FACILITIES

- The Falcon Inn is a gorgeous Grade II listed, mid-18th century slate fronted building, with beamed ceilings and an open fire. The outside has a stunning wisteria and magnolia that flower late spring. There is disabled access apart from toilets, being due to be a listed building, wheelchair users need to use the nearby public facilities. This Free House serves food, liquid refreshments including coffee and tea. A beer festival is held in July.
www.thefalconinnstmawgan.co.uk

- The Village Store/Post Office also has a delightful tearoom to its rear in an immaculate garden and conservatory. Access (not easy for wheelchairs) although can be via the side gate on the lane to the car park or through the shop. (There is a free to use cashpoint in the post office side of the shop.) For opening hours, refer to -
www.stmawganstoresandtearoom.co.uk

Snow drops

TR7 2NN

02

WALK 02

NEWQUAY – TRENANCE GARDENS, LEISURE PARK & BOATING LAKE

THIS AREA OF NEWQUAY IS A REAL 'LOCALS' GEM AND OFFERS SOMETHING FOR EVERYBODY. NORMALLY WHEN CONSIDERING NEWQUAY, IT'S THE BEACHES AND COASTLINE THAT SPRINGS TO MIND, WHICH ARE OFTEN DIFFICULT TO ACCESS WITH WHEELS AND CROWDED IN FINE WEATHER. HOWEVER, THIS SHELTERED, SEMI-TROPICAL VALLEY TO THE SOUTH OF THE TOWN GIVES THE OPPORTUNITY FOR A 'FIGURE-OF-EIGHT' WALK SUITABLE FOR ALL FORMS OF WHEELS AS IT'S ON TARMAC FOOTPATHS. PLEASE BE CAREFUL THOUGH AS THERE IS OPEN ACCESS TO STREAMS AND BODIES OF WATER.

DISTANCE: Easy going for all wheels approximately 2.5km/1.6 miles.

PARKING: Using the OS Explorer 104 Redruth and St Agnes 1:25000 with grid reference 819613 or SAT NAV TR7 2NN for the car park by Heron Tennis.

The easiest way to access the car park is from the south of Newquay, on the A3075 turning onto the A392 at Trevemper roundabout signposted for Newquay, and then turning right along Trevemper Road, driving straight on at the double roundabout, under the viaduct and turning right, signposted for Newquay Zoo and Waterworld. The car park is first on the left by the tennis dome and playground. Parking is usually available all year. While it may get busy during school term-time with parents picking up around 3pm, there is plenty of car parking further along the turning, in front of and behind Waterworld (behind Waterworld is nearly flat compared to the sloped area in front and adjacent).

- THE WALK -

This is a tarmac easy going walk, on the whole on the flat with a slight gradient in part. There are multiple car parking opportunities in this area. However, I start the walk at the car park adjacent to the Heron Tennis Centre. It is a Cornwall Council owned, pay and display public car park.

©Visit Newquay

When out of the vehicle and organised, have the Heron Tennis building in front of you and take the footpath to its left, under the lime trees. Walk around the outside of Heron and continue past the benches and Newquay Trenance Bowling Club. At the corner, turn right onto Wildflower Lane, following the path along the boundary of Newquay Zoo where there are glimpses of zebras and owls.

After about 250m, Wildflower Lane turns to the right, over a bridge and stream, effectively following the zoo boundary with further possible sightings of tapirs. Continue along Wildflower Lane for around 150m, up a gentle slope, before turning right again along a quiet stretch of lane that does have vehicular access to the local college, so a little care needs to be taken but there is room for vehicles and others.

This 50m stretch takes you effectively to Waterworld car park; take care crossing this and be aware of two-way traffic. The path continues to the left of the Waterworld building and starts a gentle downslope (if you have a long-base wheelchair then turn right down the hill at about 75m so you're opposite the zoo, turn left at the bottom and continue to the climbing wall) for 200m past the crazy-golf on your right and there are offset bars to stop access straight onto the road at the bottom. Go through these and turn left onto the pavement (opposite where you parked at Heron), continue along past the climbing wall on your left, over the stream and take the footpath to your right underneath the impressive granite viaduct.

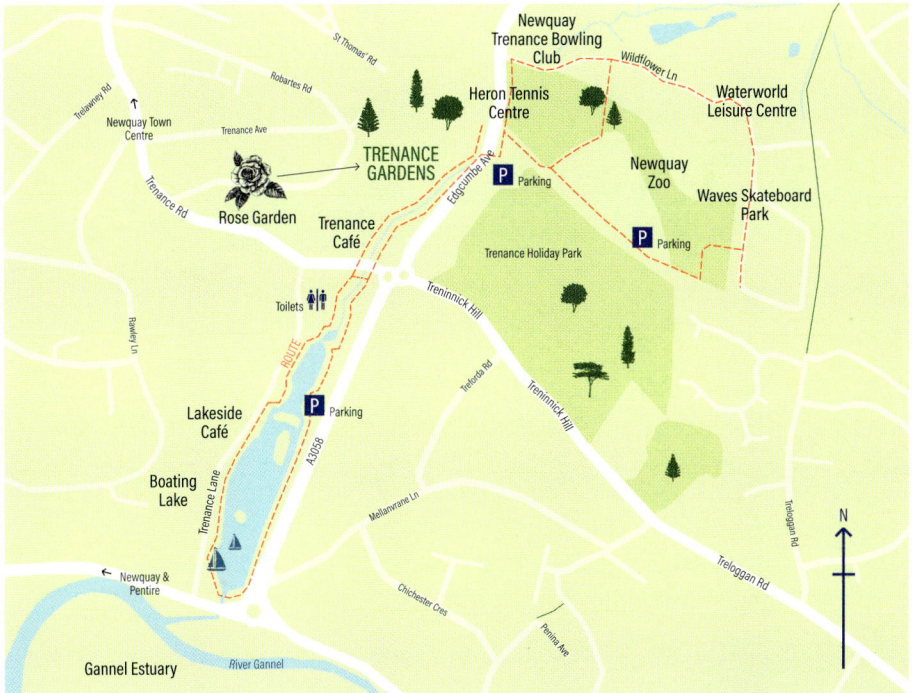

Newquay Trenance Bowling Club

Wildflower Ln

St Thomas' Rd

Robartes Rd

Trelawney Rd

Newquay Town Centre

Trenance Ave

Heron Tennis Centre

Waterworld Leisure Centre

TRENANCE GARDENS

Edgcumbe Ave

Parking

Newquay Zoo

Waves Skateboard Park

Trenance Rd

Rose Garden

Trenance Café

Trenance Holiday Park

Parking

Toilets

Treninnick Hill

Rawley Ln

ROUTE

Lakeside Café

Parking

A3058

Treforda Rd

Treninnick Hill

Boating Lake

Trenance Lane

Mellanvrane Ln

Chichester Cres

Newquay & Pentire

Pentire Ave

Treloggan Rd

Treloggan Rd

N

Gannel Estuary

River Gannel

Walk along here for 100m where there is a pelican crossing; cross over the road and take the footpath to the left. This is Trenance Gardens and home to a delightful selection of well-maintained trees, roses, herbaceous borders, annual bedding and seasonal bulb-planted lawns.

©Visit Newquay

Walk along the mid-lawn path for 200m and then use the zebra crossing to cross the road before turning right, over the stream and into the rose garden. This part of Trenance is divine in the summer with colour and smell. The pergola offers some shade if it's a sunny day and there are benches allowing everyone to sit and enjoy the view. When you're ready to continue, follow the path by the stream and lake, with public toilets on your right as well as sheltered seating.

Continue ahead and in front of Lakeside Café and all the way around the lake for approximately 400m until you reach the small causeway beside Lakeside Café. Continue along the path under the trees back towards the rose gardens and the zebra crossing. Cross back over the road but stay on the left-hand side path past old Trenance Cottages, where there is another café and a small shop. Continue under the viaduct and back to your car.

- WALK EXTENSION -

If without wheels there are various options for extended walking. At the western end of the boating lake there is pedestrian access across the A392 to The Gannel Estuary, which has footpaths along the river towards the sea, as well as crossing the river and reaching the pretty village of Crantock. Please be aware of tides and consult timetables before setting off. Take a map and it can be muddy so be suitably prepared.

other information

TOILETS: As with all of Newquay Town Council's toilets, 20p is required to enter, including the disabled facilities.

BUSES: 85 and 87 – Newquay to Truro buses have a stop by the viaduct/Newquay Zoo.

DOGS: This is a popular walk for dog walkers. Dogs must be on leads and waste bins are dotted around on route.

FREE PARKING: There is free 3 hour parking along Trevemper Road, parallel to the boating lake.

LAND TRAIN: Also on Trevemper Road is a stop for the seasonal Newquay Land Train that has a circuit around the town and is perfect for everyone using wheels. It has full disabled access for wheelchairs www.visitnewquay.org/things-to-do/newquay-land-train-p2401313

BOAT HIRE: Seasonal on the main lake by Lakeside Café.

—NATURE—

Trenance Gardens is a delight for gardeners and was the inspiration of John Ennor, who took on unemployed men during the 1930s depression in exchange for a hot meal a day (usually a pasty!) to build the site. Spring comes early, blooming with a selection of hellebore (Christmas roses), various magnolia, carpets of anemones and crocuses, ornamental cherries and narcissi. There is also a stunning display of fritillaries in the grass in the right-hand side corner just exiting the boating lake gardens before the zebra crossing. Flower beds have seasonal bedding around permanent exotics.

The rose garden is home to 1900 roses consisting of 50 species of rambling, hybrid teas, climbing, floribundas, bourbon, old English and other shrub roses.

There are various waterfowl and gulls to be spotted at the lake, including glossy ibis which apparently come into roost on the island at dusk. Please don't feed the birds bread though as it has no nutritional value for them but effectively fills them up; Lakeside Café sell small bags of bird food.

There are some large fish to be spotted in the lake and stream but take care near the water.

what's nearby

Newquay Zoo www.newquayzoo.org.uk - a small zoo that is part of the Paington Zoo group.

Blue Reef Aquarium www.bluereefaquarium.co.uk/newquay - a small impressive aquarium by the harbour in the middle of town.

Waterworld Leisure Centre - www.better.org.uk/leisure-centre/cornwall/waterworld - for a fun pool, 25m standard pool, gym and various fitness classes.

©Visit Newquay

FACILITIES

- Heron Tennis Centre is open to the public and has a café. www.heron-tennis.co.uk
- There is a small café being refurbished in the car park by the Heron Tennis Centre.
- The Lakeside Café (also a restaurant) and Trenance Cottages both sell good ice creams, snacks and meals. www.lakesidenewquay.co.uk, www.trenancecottages.co.uk/cafe.html
- Free facilities include a young children's play space by Heron Tennis Centre, whilst older children have access to a climbing area between Heron car park and the viaduct as well as Concrete Waves Skatepark behind Waterworld.
- There is a seasonal crazy golf course and a miniature railway for rides.

Towan Head

WALK 03

NEWQUAY – TOWAN HEAD

TOWAN HEAD, NEWQUAY, OFFERS SOME OF THE MOST SPECTACULAR COASTAL SCENERY THAT I HAVE EVER SEEN. ON A CLEAR DAY THE VIEW IS STUNNING, ESPECIALLY WITH A CLEAN-GLASSY SWELL COMING IN FROM THE ATLANTIC, DRIVING SURFERS' DREAM WAVES ONTO THE CRIBBAR AND THE ICONIC FISTRAL BEACH.

Fistral Beach

DISTANCE: A short walk approximately 2km/just under 1.5miles.

PARKING: SAT NAV TR7 1HL for the Cornwall Council seasonal pay and display car park at the top of Dane Road, opposite the Atlantic Hotel or using the OS Explorer 104 Redruth and St Agnes with grid reference 806622. To get to the Dane Road car park, follow signage to Fistral beach and you will probably end up driving along Tower Road with Newquay golf course on your left. You will come to a mini roundabout with the Red Lion Inn opposite; take the turning towards your left, continue up the hill (Dane Road) and on towards the Atlantic Hotel.

The car park is at the top of the hill, on your left, just before the road becomes one-way curving to the right and continuing round to circumnavigate the Atlantic Hotel and come out behind the Red Lion Inn.

- THE WALK -

An easy-going surface (half is tarmac and the rest is a fine compact gravel) for all wheels but with two short steep sections including a piece of quiet one-way road.

When ready, with all the usual preparations, leave the car park and continue up the rest of the hill on the same side of the road for approximately 100m. This quiet, one-way road (King Edward Crescent) goes all the way around the Atlantic Hotel clockwise. Follow this road to the right for another 150m if you wish to see the Huer's Hut. This 14th century white-washed small building was used by fishermen to spot shoals of pilchards and to give directions to the fishermen when at sea as to where the shoals would be located; a beautiful and fascinating Newquay historical feature.

After visiting the Huer's Hut, if you wheel and go back up the road to the tarmac path on your right, take this and wheel all the way down to the bottom of the hill for a further 600m, where it meets a small road that goes to Towan Head

car park. You could continue to Towan Head car park if there are wheel-less members on your walk, and they could walk up to the top of the headland to the shelter which commands amazing views up and down the coast. Sadly, there is no wheel access to the top.

Also in the car park is the old lifeboat station, erected in the 1800s and in use until 1934. At the time it had the steepest slipway in Britain with a 1:2 ¼ gradient. Today the artist Nicholas Williams uses the building as a studio and has an intriguing porthole in the door to observe what is going on outside.

If you're not going on to Towan Headland, then carefully cross the road to the compressed gravel track that leads around the left and the edge of the self-catering complex and along the coast

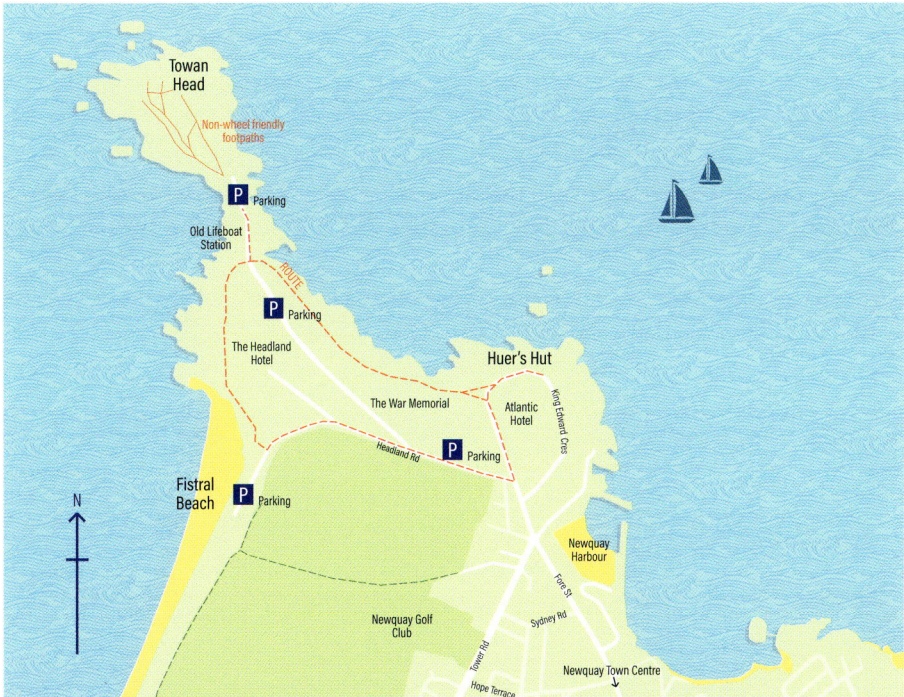

towards Fistral Beach. Follow the path to the Fistral Beach Complex (450m) where you can pause to shop, use the facilities or grab something to eat.

Now you can either retrace your route, or leaving the complex, wheel up the road, taking care, and then wheel along Headland Road on the wide promenade pavement to the end (approximately 500m). Once here, cross the road and turn left back up the short steep hill of Dane Road to the car park (approximately 70m).

Huer's Hut

- WALK EXTENSION -

If you're wanting a really long wheel (6km/3.7 miles round trip) and you have all-terrain wheels then you can, from Dane Road car park, go down the hill to the mini roundabout. Bear right and go all along Tower Road to the large roundabout, turn right along Pentire Road and turn right onto the Esplanade. Wheel to the end where the road finishes and a rough track goes up the hill, hugging the coast and meeting the tarmac lane (vehicular access with passing places) down to the Lewinnick Lodge for good beer, food and fine views of Fistral from the southern end.

other information

TOILETS: Are available seasonally at Towan Head car park and at the Fistral Beach Complex.

BUSES: Newquay bus station is in the centre of the town approximately 800m away from the start of the walk.

DOGS: Fistral Beach is dog friendly and waste bins are dotted around on route.

FREE PARKING: Is seasonal pay and display. At Dale Road there is limited free on-road parking on surrounding roads. If a customer at the big hotels, then they have car parking too.

OTHER: Newquay Land Train – www.newquay.co.uk/the-newquay-road-train for map, getting off at stop 'L' and wheeling down the lower half of Tower Road and joining the walk on Dane Road. It has full disabled access for wheelchairs www.visitnewquay.org/things-to-do/newquay-land-train-p2401313 but is seasonal from the beginning of April to the end of October.

Nicholas Williams (Old Lifeboat Station Studio) – www.nicholascwilliams.co.uk

Headland Hotel

—NATURE—

There is good viewing of seabirds – gannets, cormorants, gulls and shags as well as other birds such as kestrels. Seals and dolphins can sometimes be seen. West Pentire Head (where the Lewinnick Lodge boutique inn/hotel is situated) has had short-eared owls as regular winter visitors. I have seen an all-terrain wheel based bird-watcher follow the path from the car park to the end of Pentire Headland to view these gorgeous birds hunting at dusk.

what's nearby

Lappa Valley www.lappavalley.co.uk - Cornwall's secret trains - steam engines for everyone!

Cornwall Aviation Centre
www.cornwallaviationhc.co.uk - an amazing array of jet fighters and bombers all available to see up close.

Perranporth - 13km/8miles, this small coastal resort town has cafés, some shops, car parking, wide pavements and is basically on the flat with access to the huge beach, recently made popular by being one of the main coastal settings for the recent BBC Poldark series.

FACILITIES

- Fistral Beach Complex - www.fistralbeach. co.uk/the-fistral-beach-complex has a variety of shops and eateries. There are toilets and hot showers (small charge for the latter) and beach wheelchair hire from Fistral Beach Surf Hire (surfboards may be hired too). There are many events through the year so check the website for details or times to avoid the area as it can get very busy. There is disabled parking by the complex in the large pay and display car park (free after 6.30pm) if you wish to start here as a location. Fistral Beach is dog friendly all year round.
- Use the 'webcam' menu on the website for detailed surf and weather accounts for the day and near future as it is well worth referring to before wheeling out.
- Atlantic Hotel - www.atlantichotelnewquay.co.uk - for dining and afternoon tea.
- Headland Hotel - www.headlandhotel. co.uk - for dining and afternoon tea.
- Lewinnick Lodge - www.lewinnicklodge. co.uk - good beer, excellent food and cream teas.

04

Bluebells at Tehidy

WALK 04

TEHIDY COUNTRY PARK

THE HISTORY OF THE TEHIDY ESTATE IS FASCINATING. IT'S REFERRED TO IN THE POLDARK SERIES, WITH THE BASSET FAMILY MAKING THEIR FORTUNE WITH METAL MINING IN THE 18TH AND 19TH CENTURIES, A COMPREHENSIVE DESCRIPTION CAN BE FOUND AT WWW.HOUSEANDHERITAGE.ORG/2019/04/05/TEHIDY. SADLY, THE ORIGINAL HOUSE WAS DAMAGED BY FIRE AND THE BAROQUE STYLE HOUSE IS NOW CONVERTED TO PRIVATE APARTMENTS FROM THE OLD COUNTY TB HOSPITAL. NOW YOU CAN JUST SEE TANTALISING GLIMPSES OF THE CLOCK TOWER AND THE OLD CARRIAGE ENTRANCE TO THE STABLE BLOCK VIA AN AVENUE.

TEHIDY COUNTRY PARK (250 ACRES) IS NOW A CORNWALL COUNCIL RURAL ESTATE, 3KM TO THE NORTH OF CAMBORNE.

DISTANCE: Various distances depending on the route taken.

PARKING: SAT NAV TR14 0EZ for free parking at the country park but it can fill up, especially on a fair weather Sunday.

Waterfall at Tehidy

- THE WALK -

These are various short walks of 1km or less that although indicate are for disabled access would be better suited to all-terrain buggies as the surface is poor and can be extremely muddy after rain. The main walk for wheels is on the flat around the lake which has a wide range of tame water fowl.

Take the Pool, Camborne, A3047 Portreath turn off the A30, if coming from the east then take the right-hand lane from the slip road and turn right at the traffic lights, pass under the A30, turn left on the bend and follow the signage to Tehidy Country Park. SAT NAV TR14 0EZ – will get you to the area and then follow signage. OS Explorer 104 Redruth and St Agnes with grid reference 649433.

I have drawn a map, however Cornwall Council produce a comprehensive map of the Country Park that highlights the walks suitable for wheels and can be printed out beforehand - www.cornwall.gov.uk/media/3625017/Tehidy-Country-Park-Map.pdf.

The park is open dawn to dusk. Dog access is restricted to walks away from the lakes.

Note: when visited in the autumn the paths were fairly muddy and an all-terrain set of wheels is required after rain.

Porcelain Fungus

Dogs are allowed away from the lakes

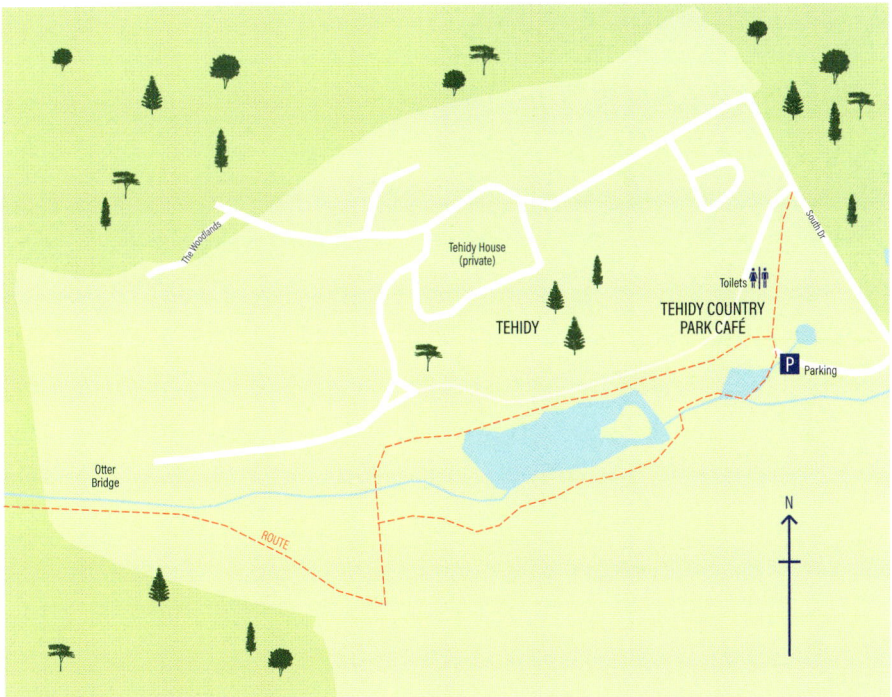

other information

TOILETS: Including disabled, are free at the rear of the café.

BUSES: 47 – Camborne/Redruth service that stops at the outer edge (Eastern Lodge) of Tehidy Park and would then involve a long wheel of 1.2km/0.7m to get to the café.

DOGS: Specific routes are designated for dog walking. There are other routes around the lake where dogs are banned.

FREE PARKING: There is free parking at the country park but it can fill up, especially on a fair weather Sunday.

what's nearby

Trevince House – Gwennap, Redruth, TR16 6BA www.trevince.co.uk - is another estate, gardens and café. This is open from late March to late September.

Heartlands – between Pool and Redruth TR15 3QY www.heartlandscornwall.com - a free attraction based upon a previous mining site. There are cafés, arts and crafts workshops, giant-adventure play-space all within the 19 acre site.

Portreath - small coastal harbour village just to the north of Tehidy.

—NATURE—

As the estate has parkland and lakes it has become a haven for birds. There are plenty of friendly birds but please avoid feeding them bread, instead offer them seed or corn from a pet or agricultural shop.

FACILITIES

- There is a café at the free car park that is open 6 days a week (closed Monday) 10am to 4/5pm depending on time of year. Public toilets, including a disabled toilet, are behind the café and are open dawn to dusk.

Copperhouse Pool

WALK 05

HAYLE – COPPERHOUSE POOL

THIS IS FOR YOUR WHEELING BIRDWATCHER AND FOR THOSE WHO ARE LOOKING FOR A PLEASANT WHEEL IMMERSION IN AN ECHO OF HAYLE'S PAST METAL-BASED INDUSTRIAL HERITAGE. BINOCULARS WOULD BE USEFUL.

♿ **DISTANCE:** Easy going for all wheels, flat tarmac and compressed gravel approximately 3km/1.8miles.

P **PARKING:** SAT NAV TR27 4BL for Hayle outdoor swimming pool car park or OS Explorer 102 Land's End with grid reference 558377.

King George V Memorial Walk

King George V Memorial Walk next to Copperhouse Pool

- THE WALK -

The basic walk is a circumnavigation of Copperhouse Pool that was originally constructed as a tidal reservoir to allow shipping to pick up copper from the adjacent metal smelting works back in the 1700s. It can be taken as a circular walk or a 'there and back again' experience just along the King George V Memorial section. As with all walks adjacent to water, take care!

If coming down the A30 from Camborne/Redruth turn right at the large roundabout for Hayle town centre. Drive straight on at the next roundabout, driving along the south side of Copperhouse Pool for about 2km then turn right (there is a middle lane to let you do this) signposted for North Quay and Beaches. Cross the bridge, and after approximately 150m, turn right and the car park is just past the café on the corner. (The café inside is tiny and not suitable for wheels, although in fine weather there is outdoor seating on the flat.)

When ready to leave the car park, suitably attired for the weather (there is no real shelter on this route) and with the car park behind you, turn right along the footpath by the 'Access Only' road, along the 1km long King George V Memorial Walk. Most people I have seen on this route walk along the road as there is very little traffic but the separate 'walk' is present if you wish to feel safer. The walk has benches for a pause and has areas of shrub and Mediterranean type herbaceous planting.

At the end of Copperhouse Pool, (approximately 1km/0.6miles) the footpath straight ahead is fine for all-terrain buggies, especially if you wish to visit the play park (there is a step at the end); for other wheels, and an easier gravel path, turn right here. This path hugs the eastern end of Copperhouse Pool and after about 400m reaches a small road (Lethean Lane). If a playground/skateboard park and/or toilet facilities are needed turn right here and cross the road opposite the seasonal café (white building) by the off-road car parking and on the right is the entrance to the park and access to the toilets including disabled. If a facility stop has occurred, then return back down Lethean

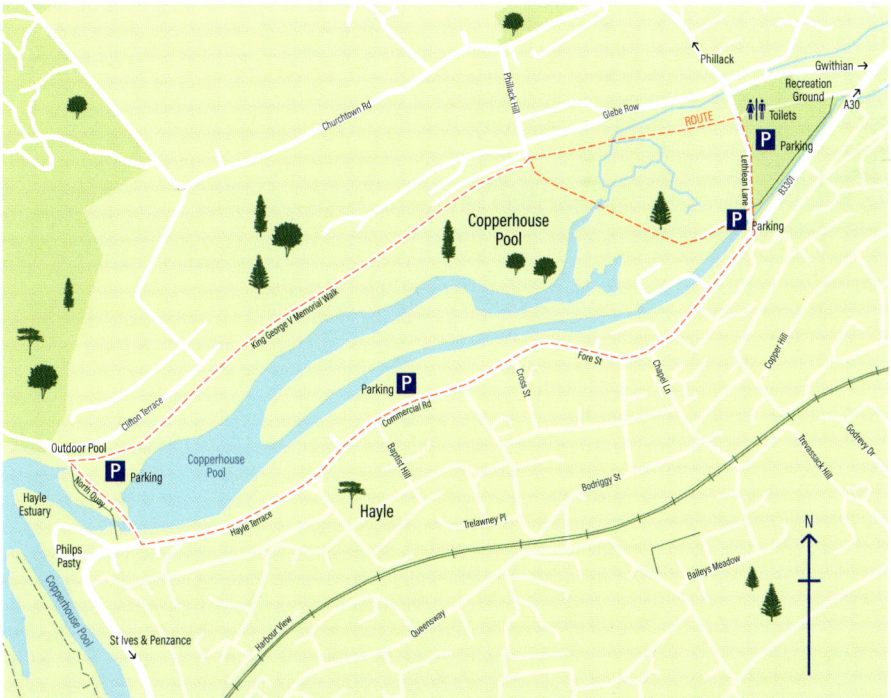

Lane, now you could return to the car the way you came or continue along to the main road and turn right for the circular route.

This road is Hayle's main high street, busy with traffic, a variety of shops, restaurants, pubs and the well-sited Hayle library. It is well worth popping into the library (approximately 700m on the right on Commercial Road) to read the daily newspaper in the community garden over-looking Copperhouse Pool.

Past the library and in another 600m there are traffic lights where you turn right back over the bridge and North Quay to the car park.

- WALK EXTENSION -

Approximately 3km/1.8 miles
For those with all-terrain-wheels, and on a calm day with children safely secured, instead of crossing the bridge back to the car park, follow the road around to the left and along Penpol Terrace and effectively the B3301. If a snack is required, you'll find Philps Pasty shop and café (with a car park) opposite. Continue along the road for approximately 300m where, just before the viaduct, cross the road and proceed along the path under the viaduct, baring right and back under the viaduct wheeling past ASDA. Take the turning into Asda (car park, café and toilet facilities if needed) and, having crossed the road at the traffic lights and wheeled for approximately 90m along the road, turn left onto the footpath and continue along the old East Quay, heading into Hayle Estuary and amidst the RSPB reserve. This is a dangerous place for unsupervised small children and dogs, as the water currents around this promontory can be treacherous, so extra care needs to be taken.

This area is definitely one to look at but not touch as it gives an amazing experience of being surrounded by water, alongside spectacular views over towards Lelant and out to sea.

other information

TOILETS: Free public toilets at Lethean Lane recreation grounds and Foundry Square by the viaduct.

BUSES: The frequent T1 (Penzance to Truro), T2 (St Ives to Truro) and the infrequent Atlantic Coaster St Ives to Newquay. www.firstgroup.com

DOGS: This is a popular walk for dog walkers. Dogs must be on leads and waste bins are dotted around on route.

FREE PARKING: There is free parking in the car park where you start as well as Lethean Lane by the playground and in Hayle though disabled access can become more vexing.

OTHER: There is a skateboard park located in the recreation park at Lethean Lane.

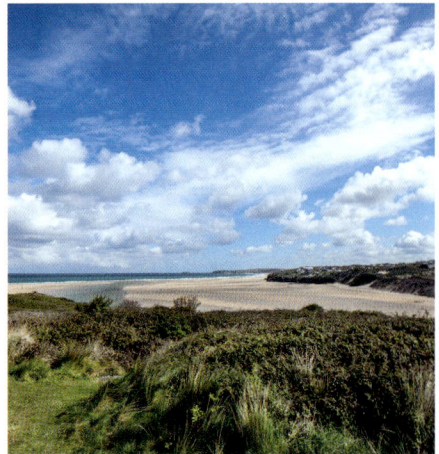

View from Lelant

—NATURE—

Common Snipe

Copperhouse Pool and the Hayle Estuary are excellent for spotting various seabirds. Check www.cbwps.org.uk/cbwpsword/sightings for recent sightings or look at the RSPB bird identifier for help www.rspb.org.uk/birds-and-wildlife/wildlife-guides/identify-a-bird

what's nearby

Redshank

Paradise Park www.paradisepark.org.uk - primarily a bird themed zoo.

St Erth Park and Train ride to St Ives
www.gwr.com - a short but stunning GWR train journey to St Ives without the hassle of trying to park in St Ives in summer.

Godolphin House, Estate and Gardens
www.nationaltrust.org.uk/godolphin - a National Trust property approximately 7km/4.5miles to the SW of Hayle. The estate is open dawn to dusk 363 days a year, the gardens are open 10 to 5pm. Countryside Mobility along with Heritage Mobility have provided an all-terrain 'tramper', electric wheelchair to be borrowed around the estate and gardens. To book, telephone 01736 763194. For further details and opening times then check website.

FACILITIES

- Hayle Swimming Pool (lido) - is a seasonal outdoor pool that lends itself to another era and is fine for families with children but not really equipped for those dependent on their wheels and disabled facilities. www.hayleswimmingpoolfriends.org.uk

- Hayle Library and Information Centre is open Monday, Wednesday and Friday 9.30am to 5pm and Saturdays 9.30am to 12.30pm. It has a range of facilities, car parking, disabled access, daily newspapers, computers, books, DVDs and a community wildlife/reading garden overlooking the estuary. Check online at www.cornwall.gov.uk/leisure-and-culture/libraries/your-local-library/hayle-library-and-information-service

Morrab Gardens

WALK 06

PENZANCE – SEAFRONT & GARDENS (MORRAB GARDENS & PENLEE MEMORIAL PARK)

PENZANCE HAS MANY WONDERFUL CHILDHOOD MEMORIES FOR ME, AND THIS WALK OFFERS SOME DIVERSE EXPERIENCES. THE WIDE, OPEN, ORIGINALLY VICTORIAN PROMENADE MAY OFFER A CLEAR SEA VIEW OVER MOUNTS BAY TOWARDS THE LIZARD, WHEREAS THE SOUTH FACING ASPECT OF GEORGIAN AND VICTORIAN TOWN HOUSING, NARROW WALKWAYS, PARKS AND GARDENS GIVES A LOVELY SHELTERED STROLL INTO THE PAST.

Gazania

DISTANCE: Easy going for all wheels (slight inclines in places) approximately 2.5km/1.6 miles.

PARKING: SAT NAV TR18 4NQ for the Wherry Town car park on the Western Promenade Road. Use OS Explorer 102 Land's End with grid reference 468295. There are multiple on road free car parking opportunities in this area. However, these might pose as being dangerous if exiting your vehicle with wheelchairs and/ or small children, so I suggest starting the walk at the Wherry Town pay and display Cornwall Council car park at the location noted above.

- THE WALK -

This a flat wide paved walk at the start and then narrower pavement, so you can have a conversation. There is a drop to the side by the sea so small children would need guidance and care.

To access the car park, go straight on from the roundabout approaching Penzance on the A30 following the signs for Penzance town centre and the railway station. Drive hugging the coast and pass the dock on your left. Round the headland with the outdoor Jubilee Swimming Pool on your left and continue on Western Promenade Road. Drive straight on at the mini roundabout, towards Newlyn and then turn left, the car park is about 100m further on with its own slip-road.

When organised, exit the car park via the way you drove in, take the ramp up to the Promenade by the sea and simply enjoy the view. On a clear day it is stunning with blue seas and the sound of waves breaking on the beach. There is the opportunity to wheel all along the Promenade to Jubilee Pool and on around to the harbour and the cafés by the railway station. However, the walk I want to take you on means that after about 300m of the Promenade you need to cross the road at the pelican crossing, slightly to the left of the Queens Hotel. This has ramp access at the entrance if refreshments are required at an early stage. If not, then wheel past the Hotel and turn left along Morabb Road for 80m and cross at the zebra crossing. The southern entrance to Morrab Gardens is just up the hill on the right.

Morrab Gardens was established by a wealthy brewer Samuel Pidwell in 1841 and has had donations to its plant collection from Cornwall's wealthy landowners in the past. It is now supported by local nurseries. You may want to just wheel straight through the garden but I really expect that there will be a vista, a plant or two or pond that will distract you as you wheel up the gentle south facing paths to the top north entrance of the garden. There is a splendid Victorian ornate bandstand, a canon, Boer War memorial and various statues to peruse as well as the Morabb Library and community based Pengarth Day Centre for the over 57s.

When you've wheeled through the gardens and arrived at the north entrance at the top of the slope, pass through the gates and wheel along 50m of drive to a path to the left with a black Victorian lamp post on the corner. Take this path - Morrab Terrace - and wheel down the hill where there are some gorgeous houses and

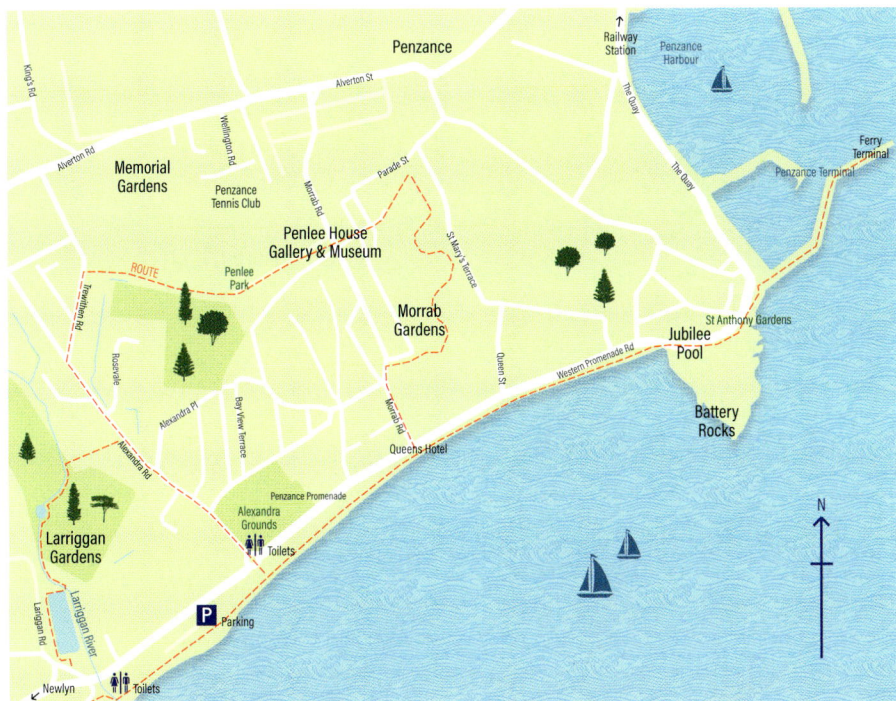

WALKS *with* WHEELS

NEWQUAY - TOWAN HEAD
- page 14 -

TEHIDY - COUNTRY PARK
- page 18 -

HAYLE - COPPERHOUSE POOL
- page 22 -

PENZANCE - LONG ROCK, MARAZION & PENZANCE
- page 32 -

PENZANCE - SEAFRONT & GARDENS
- page 26 -

HELSTON - PENROSE ESTATE
- page 36 -

Godrevy Heritage Coast
Camborne
04
St Ives
Hayle 05
Pendeen
St Just
Penzance
06
Marazion 07
Helston
08
Porthleven
Penwith Heritage Coast
Mousehole
Sennen
Porthcurno
Mullion

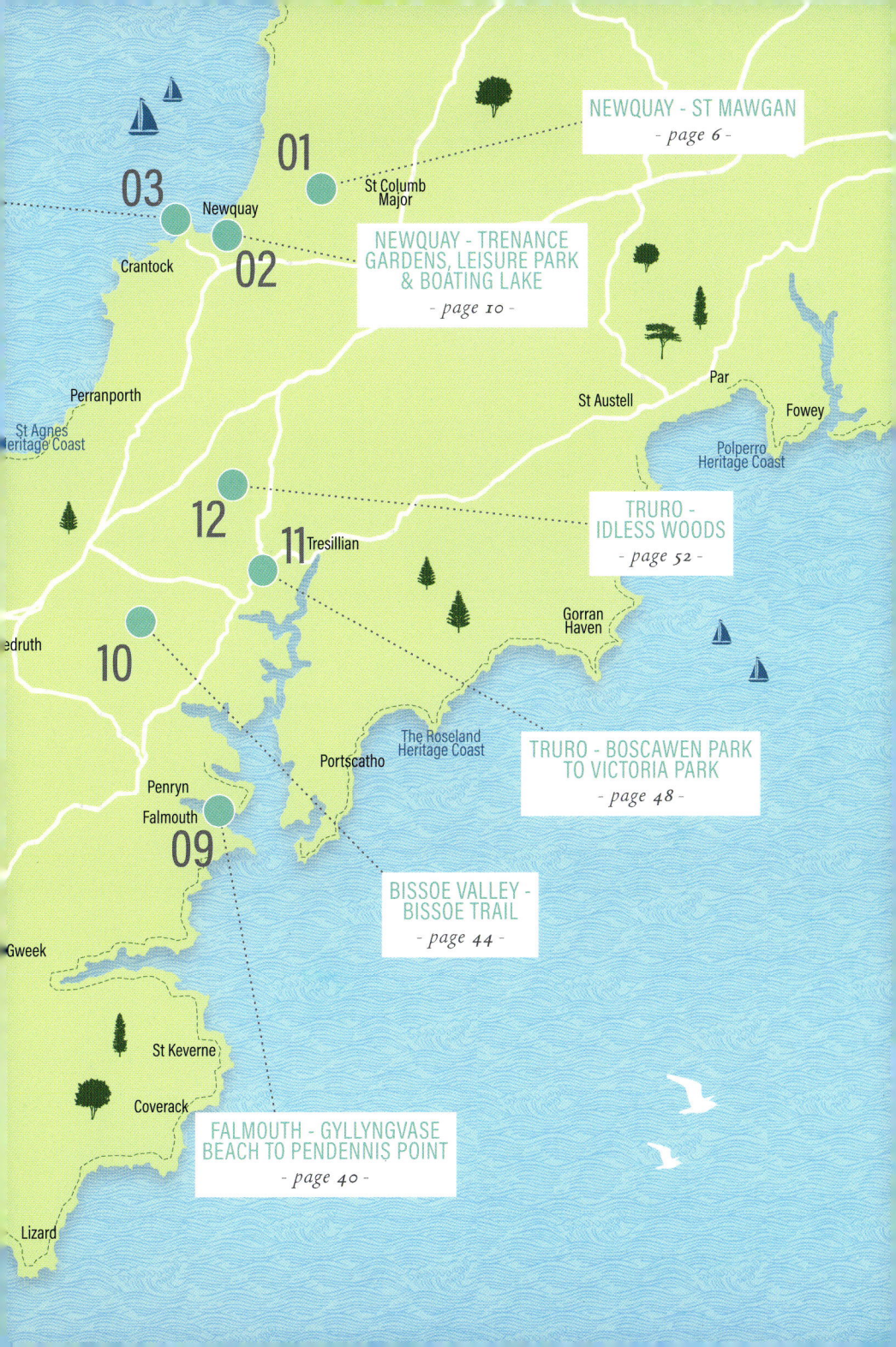

NEWQUAY - ST MAWGAN
- page 6 -

01

St Columb
Major

03

Newquay

Crantock

02

**NEWQUAY - TRENANCE
GARDENS, LEISURE PARK
& BOATING LAKE**
- page 10 -

Perranporth

St Agnes
Heritage Coast

St Austell

Par

Fowey

Polperro
Heritage Coast

12

11 Tresillian

**TRURO -
IDLESS WOODS**
- page 52 -

edruth

10

Gorran
Haven

Portscatho

The Roseland
Heritage Coast

**TRURO - BOSCAWEN PARK
TO VICTORIA PARK**
- page 48 -

Penryn

Falmouth

09

**BISSOE VALLEY -
BISSOE TRAIL**
- page 44 -

Gweek

St Keverne

Coverack

**FALMOUTH - GYLLYNGVASE
BEACH TO PENDENNIS POINT**
- page 40 -

Lizard

gardens to mosey by. The path widens out after 50m and there is vehicular access to cross over, so be careful but keep going for another 60m before reaching Morrab Road again. Cross at the zebra crossing in front of you and enter Penlee Memorial Park via the granite pillared gates.

Here in front of you is Penlee House Gallery and Museum with a great café and disabled parking. My mother was thrilled to find some past family memorabilia in the museum when we visited for her 80th birthday treat. It is amazing what these small local museums have to offer. Just past Penlee House is Penlee Park Outdoor Theatre which has various summer productions.

Very nearby is the Penzance Jewish Cemetery which is said to be the finest (of the 50 examples) outside London with headstones dating back to the mid-1700s. It is private and enclosed but at www.penzancetowncouncil. co.uk/council-services/penzance-jewish-cemetery information is given about accessing this fascinating site.

At the north end of Penlee Memorial Park is Penzance Tennis Club www.penzancetennisclub. co.uk which has a café/bar that's open to the public as well as its courts. If not distracted by the facilities in the park then you can wheel the 360m on under huge mature trees, spot squirrels and wheel down the gentle hill, past the pond and children's play area on your right, through the gate and out onto Trewithen Road. Once here turn left, wheel down 120m onto Alexandra Road, and keeping on the left-hand side down to Western Promenade Road (360m). There is a park, with shelter, play area and free public (including disabled) toilets on the corner. Cross over the Western Promenade Road by the mini roundabout and walk back along the Promenade to your vehicle (120m).

- WALK EXTENSION -

From Wherry Town car park you are able to wheel to Newlyn (approximately 1km from the car park) along the seafront and visit the Newlyn Art Gallery for a contemporary display of art works or, instead of crossing the road before the Queens Hotel, stay on the promenade to the Jubilee lido/outdoor swimming pool and on to the end of the Harbour South Pier (approximately 1.2km). If you are with a buggy, and as there are kerbs, wheel all the way round the Harbour to the end of the Albert Pier (another 1.8km from the Queens Hotel).

other information

TOILETS: Penzance has a 'community toilet scheme' as the town council has closed many public toilets – there is a map and app at www.penzancetowncouncil.co.uk/council-services/community-toilet-scheme for toilets in and around Penzance and Newlyn. There are still free disabled toilets at the bottom of Alexandra Road, in the park by the mini roundabout on the Western Promenade.

BUSES: Penzance bus station is adjacent to the railway station by the Harbour and Albert Pier. The A1 Atlantic Coaster is an open-top bus that does sight-seeing around the Penwith Peninsular and has stops on Alexandra Road and on the Western Promenade near Lidl on the way to Newlyn – check times at www.firstgroup.com/cornwall/atlantic-coasters

DOGS: This is a popular walk for dog walkers. Dogs must be on leads and waste bins are dotted around on route.

FREE PARKING: There is free parking along Alexandra Road, Trewithen Road and along the Western Promenade. There is seasonal pay and display at Wherry Town car park.

OTHER: There is a skateboard park adjacent to Wherry Town car park.

NATURE

Morrab Gardens has a stunning array of semi-tropical plants and it is possible to book a guided tour by one of the gardeners with a donation to Friends of Morrab Gardens www.morrabgardens.org.

For more information on the gardens history and for a free guide, visit - www.morrabgardens.org/wp-content/uploads/2019/05/Morrab_Gardens_Guide.pdf

Autumn and winter make the Promenade and harbour particularly good for spotting various seabirds, check www.cbwps.org.uk/cbwpsword/sightings for recent sightings.

FACILITIES

- Penlee House Gallery and Museum - www.penleehouse.org.uk - for opening times and current exhibition details. The café has a large accessible outdoor seating area, but the inside is a little cramped for wheelchair users. There is a lift to gallery floors and disabled toilet facilities are available. Please note that Penlee House is closed on Sundays, otherwise it's open 10am to 5pm in summer with earlier closing in the winter.
- Pengarth Day Centre - for the over 57s this well-established community charity offers drop-in and day car for those who want a home cooked meal, company and personal care needs. www.pengarth.co.uk/index.html or telephone 01736 364307
- Penlee Park Outdoor Theatre - www.penleeparktheatre.com

Memorial Park
©Jude Harley

what's nearby

Newlyn Art Gallery and the Exchange
www.newlynartgallery.co.uk for a contemporary look at art. Newlyn Gallery has a café with an amazing view of the Mount's Bay.

Scillonian III trips to the Isles of Scilly
www.islesofscilly-travel.co.uk/scillonian-iii to get a true feel for the exotic sub-tropical archipelago, but not for the faint hearted who are not keen on boats or who get seasick easily.

St Michael's Mount

WALK 07

PENZANCE – LONG ROCK, MARAZION & PENZANCE

THE FOCUS FOR THIS WALK IS THE VIEW OF ST MICHAEL'S MOUNT - PROBABLY CORNWALL'S MOST ICONIC VISTA! THIS IS A FAIR WEATHER WALK FOR THOSE ON WHEELS, AS BEING AN OPEN LANDSCAPE WITH NO SHELTER, NO SEATING AND A HUGE SKY. IT IS PRONE TO OUR PREVAILING SOUTH WESTERLY WIND AND EXPOSURE TO ANY RAIN/SHOWERS. CHECKING THE WEATHER FIRST AND TAKING SUITABLE PRECAUTIONS BEFORE STARTING IS A GOOD IDEA FOR THIS ALL-OUT WHEEL TO PENZANCE. THIS WALK IS FOR BOTH SERIOUS WHEELERS AND FOR THOSE WHO PREFER A BRIEF JOURNEY.

DISTANCE: Approximately 7km/4.3miles there and back again (if walking all the way to Penzance).

PARKING: SAT NAV TR17 0AA for the Station car park on the Long Rock to Marazion road. Use OS Explorer 102 Land's End with grid reference 507314.

Long Rock Beach

- THE WALK -

Flat, easy going on a compacted fine grit and concrete surface for all wheels, wide and sociable. Beware with children as there are drops in places near the beach.

This is a Cornwall Council pay and display car park with a café and café-maintained free toilets including disabled. I chose this site to start as there isn't any free parking in the area and this car park has a tarmac surface compared to the grass ones at Marazion. You could start your walk at the Penzance end at the large pay on exit car park adjacent to the railway station, bus station and harbour (SAT NAV TR18 2LL, Land's End Explorer 102 1:25000 grid ref 477305) and catch the bus to Station car park and wheel back or vice versa.

To access the Station car park, coming down the A30 and Hayle, you will have driven through Crowlas; after 1.5km (nearly a mile) there will be a large roundabout, take the second turning for Marazion (almost straight on). There is a large Cheshire Home on the left and in 0.5km the road rises to go over the main rail line out of Cornwall. Turn left and the station car park and café are right in front of you turning almost immediately right. This is a car park with a fine view of the Mount and Mount's Bay as a whole. I don't normally like the whole flask of tea and a pasty sitting in the car as my grandparents used to do but on this occasion I would make an allowance

and do just that and enjoy a car picnic taking in the view of Mount's Bay. Alternatively, grab a cuppa from the fine café in the car park.

To start the walk, when prepared and facing the sea, you are going to walk to the right, along the fine grit path with the sea on the left. This is a cycle path so beware of the silent bikes! After about 1km/0.6miles and when you have the village of Long Rock on your right, there is road access to the path so beware of the odd vehicle. After about another 1.5km/0.9miles there is a footbridge to your right with ramps and steps! If you are careful with pushing wheels you could cross the railway and use the pelican crossing to access Sainsbury's and their upstairs café, which enjoys spectacular views across Mount's Bay. Otherwise just walk the distance that you are comfortable with.

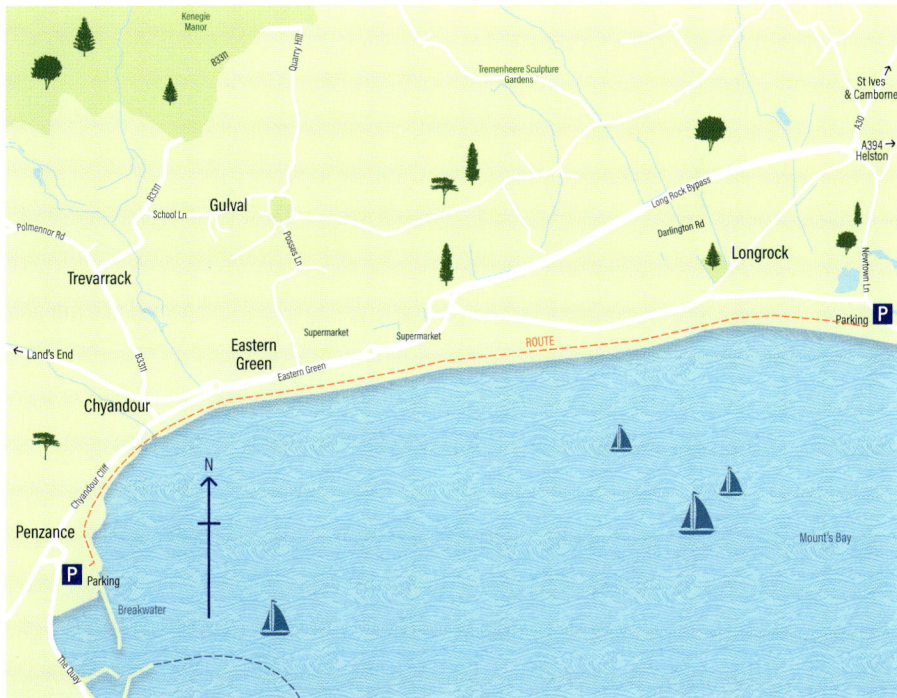

If you are a bit of a train enthusiast then Long Rock is one of the main maintenance depots for GWR, and of course Penzance station is the end and start of the line so there is plenty of opportunity for train photography, engine number gathering, new train and sleeper viewing and even the odd steam train visit.

You will reach Penzance after approximately 3.5km/2.2miles and come into the town by the railway and bus stations. There are cafés which are easily reachable over the pelican crossings while still on the flat. Of course, you could wander up into Penzance but the town itself is on an incline and it would be a struggle if pushing wheels.

If you are tired, catch the hourly A2 bus back (starting from the bus station) or if feeling like the walk, wheel back.

- WALK EXTENSION -

Starting at the station car park, you can take the cycle/walk path to your left (when facing the sea) and have the relatively short walk into Marazion and potentially wheel onto the Mount if the tide is out. Please note: this may potentially be an uncomfortable experience for those on all but the most robust all-terrain wheels, as the causeway is made from huge pieces of granite and is the equivalent to a giant's cobbled path. The causeway is also tidal and you will need to be tide-aware if attempting to get to or from the Mount otherwise you will get wet. When the tide is in there is a charged boat service that runs from Marazion to the Mount and back which could cope with buggies and folded wheelchairs if there is partial mobility.

Marazion

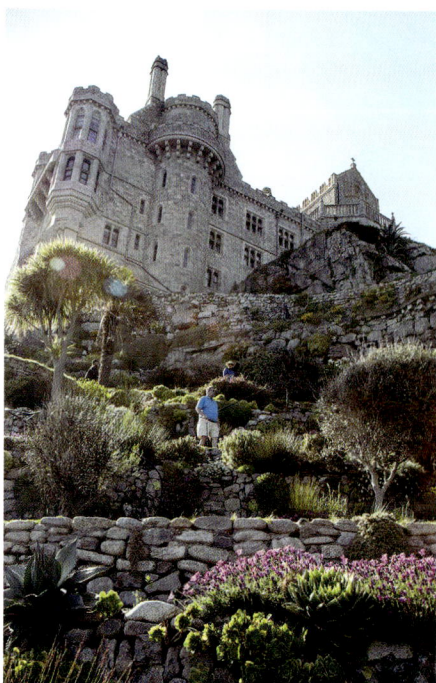

St Michael's Mount ©Matt Jessop

—NATURE—

For spotting various seabirds check www.cbwps.org.uk/cbwpsword/sightings for recent sightings. RSPB Marazion Marsh Nature Reserve is sited just to the north of Jordan's Café and car park but it is hard for those with wheels to safely observe the birds there as viewing is on the road.

Penzance

other information

TOILETS: Free, behind café in the car park.

BUSES: Penzance bus station is adjacent to the railway station by the Harbour and Albert Pier. The A2 is the hourly Penzance to St Ives bus that includes Long Rock, the station car park and Marazion on its route. Check times at www.firstbus.co.uk

DOGS: This is a popular walk for dog walkers. Dogs must be on leads and waste bins are dotted around on route.

PARKING: Is pay and display.

FACILITIES

- Café - Jordan's Café in the car park. Contact 01736 360502, for opening details.
- Watersports - paddleboards to Kayaks are available at Ocean High www.oceanhigh.co.uk which you pass just after the station car park.

what's nearby

St Michael's Mount (National Trust and St Aubyn Estates) www.stmichaelsmount.co.uk for visits to the house and gardens - both have steep sloping elements and are hard to access with wheels. However, you can wander around the harbour and there are cream teas available on the flat.

Trewidden Garden www.trewidden.co.uk has a spectacular collection of Camellia, Magnolia and tree ferns. Paths are gravelled and there is a tearoom, gift and plant shop.

Tree ferns at Trewidden Garden ©Trewidden Garden

Bluebells can be seen at Penrose Estate

TR13 0RA

08

WALK 08

HELSTON – PENROSE ESTATE

A BEAUTIFUL STROLL IN A COMFORTABLE WOODLAND BASED LANDSCAPE THAT CAN ACCOMMODATE A SELECTION OF WHEELS. HELSTON IS VERY LUCKY TO HAVE THIS FACILITY OF A LONG GORGEOUS WALK THAT IS EASILY ACCESSIBLE FOR ALL.

DISTANCE: Easy going for all wheels, flat tarmac, approximately 6km/3.7miles there and back again.

PARKING: SAT NAV TR13 0RA for the car showroom just before the car park entrance or use OS Explorer 103 The Lizard: Falmouth and Helston with grid reference 653271.

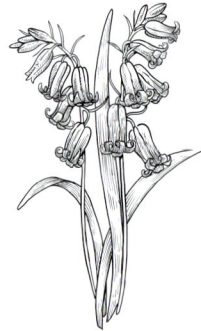

- THE WALK -

The walk is on the Penrose Estate, now owned by the National Trust (NT). It is along the original main private drive from Helston to Penrose House, on the flat parallel to the River Cober ending up adjacent to Loe Pool; Cornwall's largest fresh water lake. As with all walks adjacent to water, take care. There is no free access for motor vehicles apart from the occasional National Trust maintenance van. When organised there is a small footbridge over the River Cober from the car park, use this and turn right onto the footpath for about 30m where it meets the gated off lane to Penrose House. Once here, turn left and go as far as you wish or walk the full distance of 3km/1.8miles to the Stables Café. The walk bears around to the right just past the gatehouse; after about 300m, bear left and take the lane to the Stables Café in front of you. There are plenty of benches dotted along the route and glimpses of Loe Pool when just over halfway along.

Start the walk by crossing the footbridge and in fine dry weather, turn left and follow the footpath by the river if you have all-terrain wheels. Follow this path until there is another footbridge over the River Cober to the left, where you wheel right and join back up with the lane. This end bit can be a little muddy so beware!

- WALK EXTENSION -

If you have all-terrain wheels, and in the knowledge that the gravel path includes some inclines, you could continue on to the pretty fishing village of Porthleven, approximately 4km/2.5mikes away, and get the bus back. Note: the pavements and roads in Porthleven are narrow and not necessarily a wheel-friendly place, even though the harbour is on the flat with plenty to look at and places to eat.

If wheel-less you can easily continue towards Porthleven before reaching the coast and Loe Bar, where you can cross this shingle beach and continue back again around the lake to create a circular walk of about 10.5km/6.5miles in total.

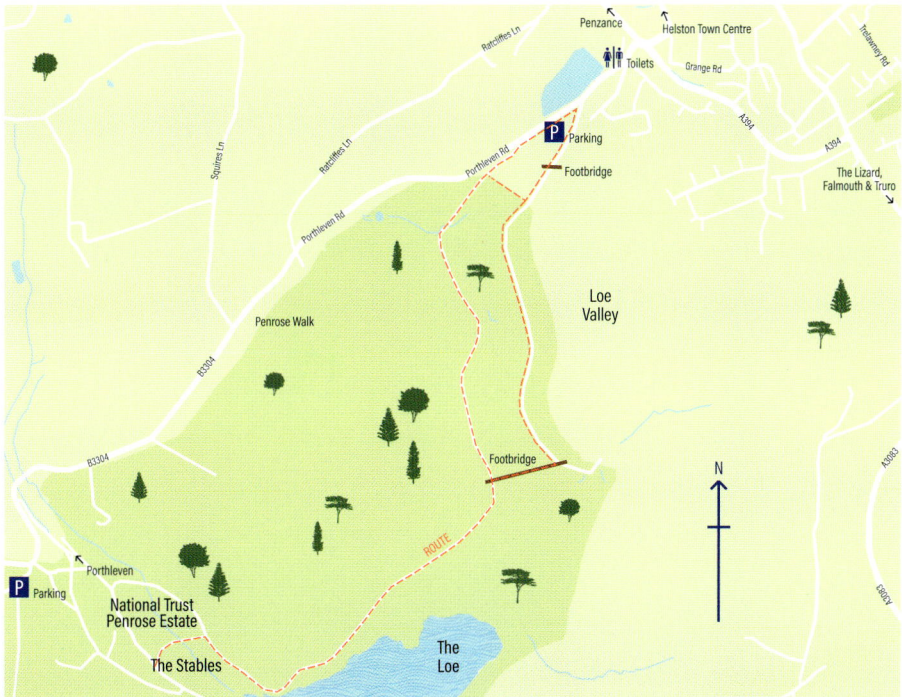

TOILETS: Free public toilets at the rear of the Lakeside Café and at the National Trust Penrose, open Easter to the end of October and weekends through the winter.

BUSES: The hourly U4 Tremough to Penzance passes through Helston and Porthleven www.bustimes.org/services/u4-tremough-helston-penzance

DOGS: This is a popular walk for dog walkers. Dogs must be on leads. Waste bins are present at the start and by the Coronation Lake.

FREE PARKING: At the start in the large gravel-based car park or pay and display car parking at the old Cattle Market - first turning to the right from the double mini roundabout off the A394.

OTHER: Play area and Skateboard park - in Coronation Park by the lake.

BIKE HIRE: at Porthleven Bike Hire adjacent to Lakeside Café.

Helston is set on a hill and does not easily lend itself to wheel access.

Flambards Theme Park
www.flambards.co.uk is just to the east of Helston, check it's website for opening dates and times, especially in winter.

RNAS Culdrose Airfield Viewing Area and Merlin Café (Gweek Road, Helston, TR12 6BB) 01326 565085 – for any plane enthusiasts.

Porthleven

Porthleven

Loe Bar

Coastpath at Loe Bar

Tufted Duck at Helston

—NATURE—

The Coronation Boating Lake has a range of friendly water birds including seasonal visitors such as tufted ducks may also be seen - please feed with appropriate bird food (available from the café) and not bread.

Loe Pool - is excellent for wildlife - www.cornwalls.co.uk/wildlife/birdwatching/loe_pool.htm. Local naturalist and bird specialist David Chapman has a variety of guides that would be useful if you would like to hone up those nature identification skills. Latest news is available from the National Trust re wildlife on the Penrose Estate - www.nationaltrust.org.uk/penrose - including bats, otters and barn owls.

FACILITIES

- Lakeside Café - open 9am to 5pm every day.
- The Stables Café - open daily 10am to 4pm, subject to dry weather, for tea, cakes and light snacks - both cafés are part of the Nauti Group of establishments based in Porthleven - www.nautibutice.co.uk

TR11 4DU

09

Aerial view of Falmouth

WALK 09

FALMOUTH – GYLLYNGVASE BEACH TO PENDENNIS POINT

♿ **DISTANCE:** This could be a 5km/3mile walk or longer if desired, by heading on into Falmouth town centre.

⒧ **PARKING:** SAT NAV TR11 4DU for Cornwall Council car park or OS Explorer 105 Falmouth and Mevagissey with grid reference 807317.

THIS IS A TRADITIONAL 'PROMENADE' TO WHEEL ALONG ON THE SEAFRONT FROM GYLLYNGVASE BEACH TO PENDENNIS POINT. FALMOUTH DEVELOPED AS A VICTORIAN HOLIDAY DESTINATION WITH THE ARRIVAL OF THE RAILWAY IN 1863 AND THE FALMOUTH HOTEL IS STILL PRESENT TODAY, LITTLE CHANGED FROM WHEN IT WAS BUILT TO CATER FOR THE VICTORIAN VISITOR. THERE ARE FINE SEA VIEWS FROM CLIFF ROAD WITH VIEWS OF ST ANTHONY HEAD, ST MAWES AND FALMOUTH, AS YOU WHEEL AROUND PENDENNIS POINT.

Queen Mary Garden

Falmouth Harbour

- THE WALK -

Good going for all wheels with tarmac pavement, though a little narrow in places. The pavement is beside a road all the way but has a sea vista to look out on. There is a gentle incline along from Gyllyngvase Beach before levelling out.

You can access this walk by bus and train from the 'Town' stop.

Start the walk at the pay and display car park at Gyllyngvase Beach car park as there are toilets nearby. There is free unlimited parking on the road as well as at Pendennis Point (but no toilets). To get to the car park along the A39 from Truro follow signposting for the National Maritime Museum and beaches. There is a brown sign for Town Beaches and Gyllyngvase Beach, where the car park is on the right.

When ready to wheel (note plenty of sunscreen by the sea) head to the sea, and wheel to the right of Queen Mary Gardens in front of you (a beautiful enclosed small sub-tropical garden). To access the seafront walk, turn left when you reach the beach and wheel along by the sea. Free public toilets (including disabled and baby changing bench) are 100m on the left and Gyllyngvase Beach Café is on the right.

The wide pavement has a gentle incline, before levelling and continuing for just over a 1km/0.6miles. There are various shelters on the way; some aspects of the shelters are more accessible for wheels than others. The Royal Duchy and The Falmouth Hotels are on the left for a more formal meal or cream tea with a view. At the end of the obvious seafront, the pavement narrows and wheels should cross the road and continue around Pendennis Point. Disabled car access to Pendennis Castle is 200m on the left, after this turning the road is one way with traffic coming towards you. The pavement is now narrow but continues around to Pendennis Point where there is a free car park with usually one or more ice cream vans.

Swanpool

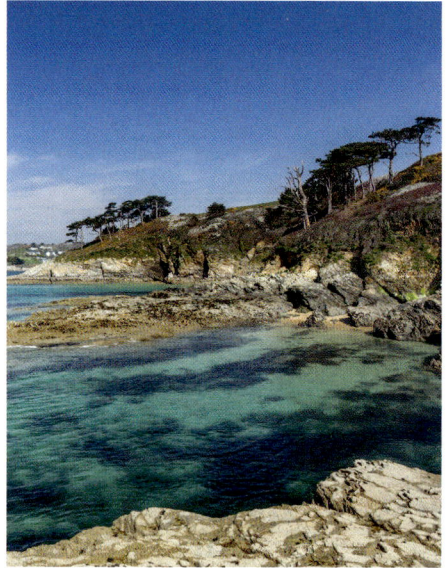
View to St Mawes from St Anthony Head

Now you can wheel back the way you have come or you can wheel on round the Point, by the road 'Castle Drive' to then face Falmouth, the port, Carrick Roads and beyond. This continues for about 1km/0.6miles, passing the access to Pendennis Castle and Ships and Castles Leisure Centre on the left. Castle Drive comes to a T-junction where you wheel to the left for 100m and join back up with Cliff Road and the seafront end of the walk to enjoy wheeling along back to Gyllyngvase.

- WALK EXTENSION -

Walk into the centre of Falmouth or continue to Swanpool and Swanpool Beach from Gyllyngvase along a narrow tarmac path (which has a few steps, so beware if you have a buggy). If you are with 4 wheels then Swanpool Beach can be reached by a small cut through from Queen Mary Road to Boscowen Road following along to the right by the pavement around Swanpool Point.

other information

TOILETS: Free public toilets, including disabled, at Gyllyngvase Beach.

BUSES: The hourly 367 operates from the bus station at Falmouth Moor to Gyllygnvase and Pendennis Point. www.bustimes.org/services/367-falmouth-town-service

DOGS: This is a popular walk for dog walkers. Dogs must be on leads and waste bins are dotted around on route.

PARKING: There is a pay and display but parking is free on the seafront and at Pendennis Point.

OTHER: GWR operate the sub 'Maritime' line between Truro and Falmouth, a stunning short train journey for further information go to www.gwr.com

— NATURE —

Binoculars would be useful as this piece of Cornish coastline offers the opportunity to spot seals around Pendennis Point and Gyllyngvase Beach. Minke and Fin whales (even the occasional humpback whale) may be seen in Falmouth Bay (April to November). A range of seabirds can be seen, typically cormorants, shags, little egret and heron being seen on shore and gannets, guillemots and razorbills occasionally coming nearer the shore. In terms of raptors, kestrel and buzzard are common and peregrines are often seen nesting around Pendennis Point.

FACILITIES

- Car parking is extensive but can be busy during the summer season.
- Further parking is available at the nearby Falmouth Town railway station and National Maritime Museum.
- There is a popular café/restaurant at Gyllyngvase beach, a few other cafés are accessible along the seafront and ice cream vans are often present at Pendennis Point.
- There are also a variety of good quality hotels such as The Royal Duchy, St Michael's and The Falmouth Hotel for lunches, cream teas and dinners, all with fine views out to sea.

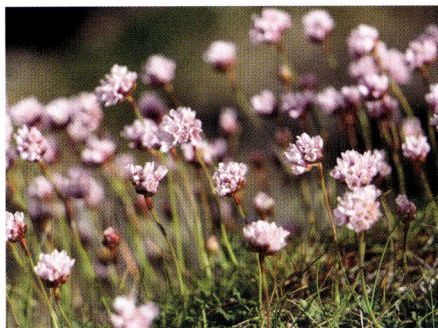

Sea Thrift

what's nearby

Falmouth town centre for shops and access to passenger ferries to St Mawes and Truro.

National Maritime Museum - www.nmmc.co.uk - has a fascinating local slant on local maritime history for all family members.

Pendennis Castle www.english-heritage.org.uk - is an English Heritage managed site that often does period events in the summer.

TR3 6PF

10

Bissoe Valley

WALK 10

BISSOE VALLEY – BISSOE TRAIL

THIS IS AN EXCEEDINGLY PRETTY AND POPULAR WHEEL AND WALK FOR PEOPLE OF ALL AGES AND WHEEL ABILITIES. IT PROVIDES A WONDERFUL OPPORTUNITY FOR YOUNG CHILDREN TO CYCLE/TRIKE ALONGSIDE AND OLDER CHILDREN TO TRY OUT THEIR MOUNTAIN BIKE SKILLS WITH THOSE WHEELING MAKING IT A REAL FAMILY EXPERIENCE.

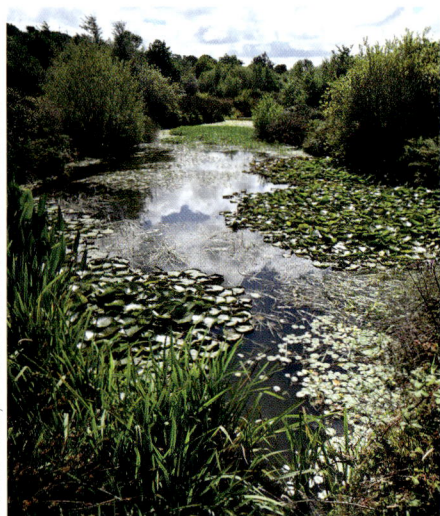

DISTANCE: Approximately up to 6km/3.75 miles there and back again.

PARKING: SAT NAV TR3 6PF or OS Explorer 105 Falmouth and Mevagissey with grid reference 790393.

Devoran Quay

Bissoe Valley Nature Reserve ©Mark Gowan

- THE WALK -

Easy going for all wheels gravel-based, flat with small road crossings and a short small road-based incline at the end. Near Bissoe the path divides – the flatter path is ideal in the summer (although can be muddy in the winter) whilst the alternative has a small eroded slope, suited to large wheels.

There is on-road parking (about 7 spaces) by taking the Devoran turn to the left roundabout, off the A39 coming from Truro (to Falmouth) 200m past the Devoran roundabout and the bottom of the dual carriageway hill. At the immediate T-junction turn right and just park along the road on the left. This is a dead-end road for cars but two-way traffic for buses. Confusing, I know, but it will become clearer when you're there. In reality you are parking on the old main road by the bus stop.

If travelling by bus, then the half-hourly U1 Falmouth to Truro has a 'Devoran Turn' bus stop right by the start of the walk and the way-marker stone for the Cycle Bissoe Trail, indicating Portreath its bridleway status.

If starting at where you park then wheel along the bus lane towards Devoran and cross the bridge, with the bus stop on your left and the start of the walk just ahead, clearly signposted. Pass under the A39 and follow the signage in the open and along the Carnon River and adjacent to a series of ponds. After 800m the trail crosses a minor road which can be busy so take care. There is an impressive view of the rail viaduct which you wheel underneath 500m after crossing the road.

There are a series of high stone-built stumps of a previous bridge besides the current viaduct and by the path is an information board explaining the history of the valley. A further 300m along is a crossing over a very minor lane that has car parking on the other side and that could be used as a halfway starting point if wished. Once here, cross over the road and continue along until there is a fork in the path, the left one is flatter but prone to flooding a little in winter and a bit

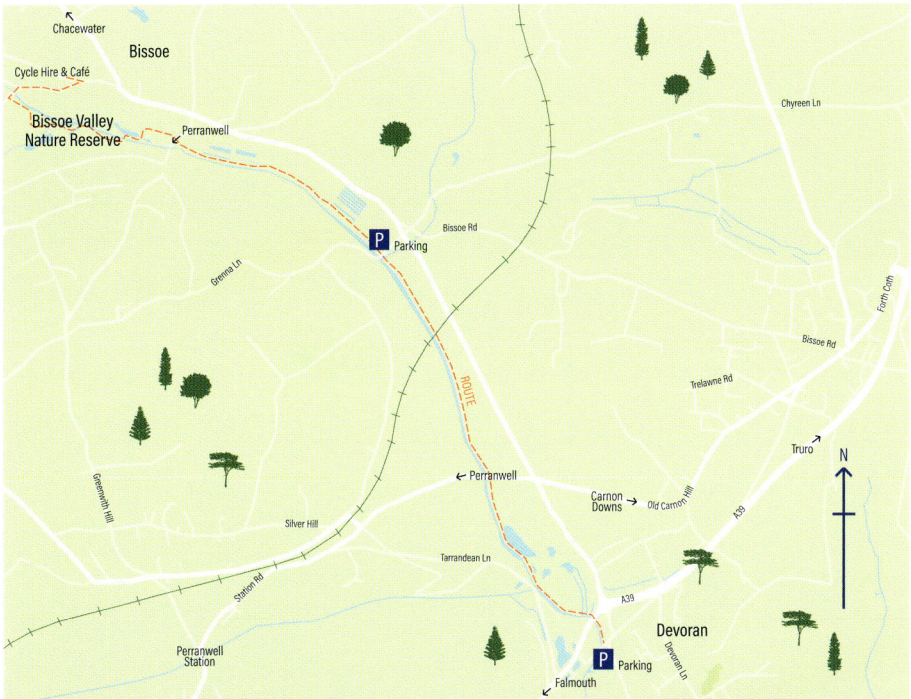

muddier, the right one has a small slope that is eroded and drier but harder to negotiate with small wheels.

Continue for a further 100m before crossing another minor lane. After about 100m the path zig-zags over the river using a wooden footbridge and continues along now on the other side of the river. The trail negotiates around a beautiful nature reserve with ponds full of native plants and, in the summer, alive with dragonflies. After this, the land opens out into a rehabilitated mine waste landscape with slopes for mountain bikes and with the old chimney still standing from the arsenic smelter.

Again, the trail meets a minor road where you turn right and there is a short wheel over the river to Bike Chain and a well-earned refreshment stop before returning.

- WALK EXTENSION -

The cycle trail itself continues along the north Cornwall coast and onto Portreath. How far you choose to go will depend on your wheels and stamina! There are some busier roads to cross but with care and attention (particularly of small children) the route to Portreath is absolutely wonderful with the added attraction of a beach at the end. Wheel and walk as far as you feel comfortable with.

Portreath

other information

TOILETS: There are toilets available at both cafés with disabled toilets available at the Bissoe Chain, Bissoe Bike Hire and Café.

BUSES: U1 Falmouth to Truro and get off at the 'Devoran Turn' there are raised kerbs at the bus stop for disabled embarkation/disembarkation – check times at www.firstgroup.com/cornwall/routes-and-maps/network-maps

DOGS: This is a popular walk for dog walkers. Dogs must be on leads and waste bins are dotted around on route.

Heron

- The Bike Chain at Bissoe (SAT NAV – TR4 8QZ) offers both bike hire and a café with gravel car parking, disabled toilet facilities. Opening daily, 9am to 5pm and extended summer opening into the evening.
www.cornwallcyclehire.com

—NATURE—

Bissoe Valley Nature Reserve is adjacent to the end of the walk by Bissoe Chain, Bissoe Bike Hire and Café - www.cornwallwildlifetrust.org.uk/nature-reserves/bissoe-valley. The Cornwall Wildlife Trust boasts this site as an excellent example of environmental conservation work with the scarce blue-tailed damselfly and the grayling butterfly establishing themselves in the ponds, woodland and heathland.

It is the best walk that I have experienced for the variety of bird species seen. In a short period of time and on one visit I have spotted a flock of long-tailed tits, heron, little egret, buzzard being chased off by a jay, greater-spotted woodpecker, great and blue tits and geese flying overhead in formation.

what's nearby

National Trust Trelissick House Gardens - www.nationaltrust.org.uk - the gravel paths at Trelissick can be wheeled. They have a bookable electric mobility vehicle and wheelchairs to borrow.

The King Harry Ferry (adjacent to Trelissick) and a drive down the Roseland Peninsula and visit the delightful villages of St Just in Roseland and St Mawes - www.falriver.co.uk/ferries/king-harry-ferry

Take the Great Western Railway 'Maritime Line' branch-line train from Truro to Falmouth and experience the view from the top of the Carnon Viaduct - www.gwr.com/plan-journey/train-times

Victoria Park

WALK 11

TRURO – BOSCAWEN PARK TO VICTORIA PARK

APART FROM BEING A GREAT COUNTY SHOPPING CENTRE, TRURO OFFERS A VARIETY OF SCENIC ENVIRONMENTS. IT IS EASY TO FORGET THAT TRURO WAS ONCE A THRIVING PORT AND THAT BY DEFINITION COASTAL, SO THIS WALK, FOR ALL WHEELS, IS A REMINDER OF THIS AND GIVES A VIEW TO HISTORIC TRURO VIA A BEAUTIFUL ROUTE.

DISTANCE: Approximately 5.5km/3.4miles (or could be two walks if parking at Garras Wharf car park and taking the pavement to Trafalgar Roundabout and then through town or turning right to Boscawen Park).

PARKING: SAT NAV TR1 1SG – for Boscawen Park car park or use OS Explorer 105 Falmouth and Mevagissey with grid reference 835437.

Along the A39 from the east drop down Tregolls Road into Truro until Trafalgar Roundabout, take the second exit signposted to Malpas and drive for about 1.6km and then turn right at the mini roundabout for the tennis courts and Boscawen Park car park (free when visited). There is also free parking along the road if you can find a space.

- THE WALK -

An easy walk for all wheels (with a small variance for wheelchairs to cope with the odd small curb/unmade path).

Starting at Boscawen Park you are going to walk back towards Truro and Trafalgar Roundabout for about 900m, along the estuary. Unfortunately, if you are in a wheelchair you will need to cross the road after about 250m as the tarmac pavement runs out (there is a small island in the road to cross to); you should be fine to continue with a buggy. The views are very different depending on high or low water; if high, then there are beautiful reflections, if low then a greater birding opportunity.

If you are in a wheelchair, cross back over the road when you are opposite the first large, white gated building on the Truro River side of the road (about a further 650m) as the pavement goes up steps and is wheels unfriendly.

Continue to the roundabout (about 360m) before bearing round to the left and going under the road using the subway. This takes you into a small garden, called Furniss Island, surrounded by the River Allen. You will be following the 'River Walk' for 75m towards the Cathedral, over the footbridge and through the buildings onto New Bridge Street. If you are with a buggy then carefully cross this one-way road (from your left), walk over the bridge and continue with the River Walk opposite. If you are a wheelchair user, then take the pavement to the left, cross the bridge, taking care as the kerb is lower a few meters down, across the road and come back again. Take the River Walk to the left, through the bollards and before the bridge you have just crossed.

Follow the river, walk across the footbridge towards the car park, and follow the footpath to the left, walking through the buildings onto Old Bridge Street. Turn left, go over the bridge before crossing the road and following the River Walk path past the bollard. The River Allen is on your right and there is a delightful section of walk where the water falls over a couple of weirs creating a relaxing sound.

Follow the path around to the left; the Cathedral and Chapter House are on your left as well as the Cathedral Café if sustenance is required.

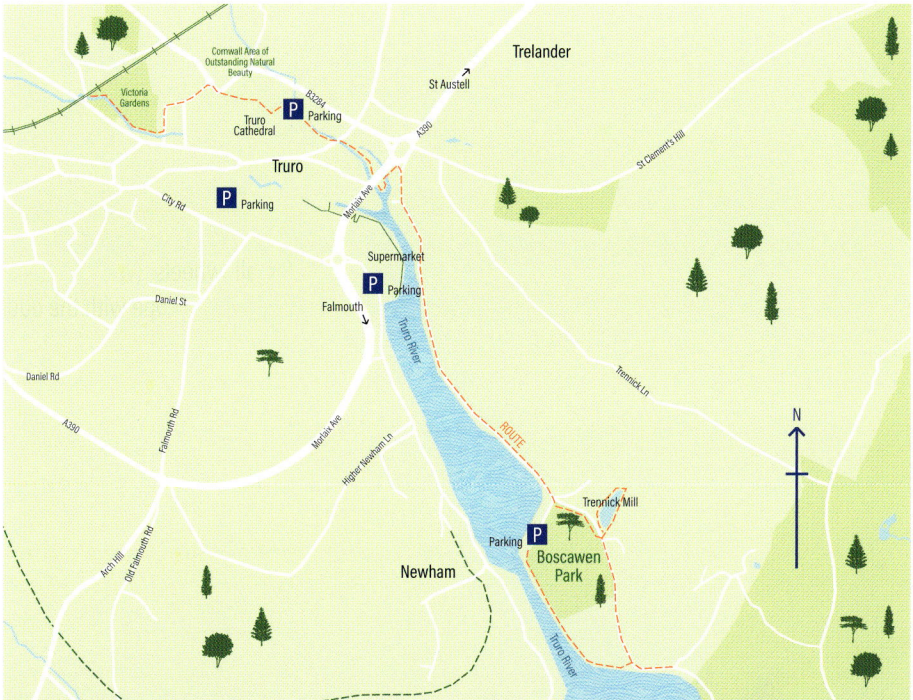

After 75m the path divides and you should wheel to the right and wheel/walk to Union Place with the impressively large Methodist Church in front of you. Follow the path to the left (vehicles do have access to this space so take care) and continue with the library on your right, crossing over the pedestrianised Pydar Street and into the alley Coombies Lane. Wheel along here until you reach the very quiet road called The Leats (to the left there are free public conveniences which may be used, as the ones later in Victoria Park are not ideal).

There is pavement on the right-hand side but care is still needed. Wheel to the end and carefully cross straight over (onto Castle Street, beware of one-way traffic coming down the hill) through the bollards and along The Leats path (with the River Kenwyn on your left and the 'leat' on your right.

Wheel along and you will come to Edward Street (again, take care as there is one-way traffic, this time going up the hill). Carefully cross the road and follow The Leats path for approximately 40m and then take the small path to your right, crossing the leat and into Victoria Gardens. Although on a slope, it should be manageable if you take your time and zig-zag your way up to the ponds, bandstand and various sculptures. It is a beautiful space with a good collection of ornamental flowering trees, seasonal bedding as well as mature trees, all having the magnificent backdrop of the railway viaduct. It is also a great place for a picnic.

On the way back, you could reverse the walk or drop down into Castle Street, turn left along River Street and there is the Royal Cornwall Museum, next to which is Truro Arts Café where you can sit outside in fine weather or can enter for internal seating on the flat. Access to the disabled toilets is via the museum ramp entrance and then entering the café that way.

If you then mooch around Truro and are too tired to return to Boscawen Park, you could take the 496 bus (at Truro bus station opposite M&S, the Piazza) to Malpas that stops at the Park on the way (please contact Travel Cornwall 01726 861108 to check that a wheelchair friendly bus is running).

- WALK EXTENSION -

Instead of walking towards Truro you could turn your wheels the other way towards Malpas along the road. After about 750m there is no pavement for about 40m to get past a house; although the road is not busy, care needs to be taken. The pavement continues along the Truro River estuary with glorious views south across a reflective idle if high water. After about 200m the path ends at 'Sunny Corner' sheltered seating.

If you are without wheels you can walk to Malpas from Boscawen Park on the footpath that hugs the river estuary but still has the 'on-road' 40m section by-passing the house. A narrow footpath then continues towards Malpas, re-joining the road for the village (there is no pavement so take care) and here you can have a well-deserved drink at the Heron Inn if it's a fine day and watch the comings and goings of the river.

You can even continue through the village and walk to St Clement 1km/0.6miles (which has a delightful tearoom and very interesting small church) and onto Tresillian 2.3km/1.4miles with the Wheel Inn at the far end of the village.

—NATURE—

The main nature attractions for this walk are birds and some interesting garden planting by Truro City Council. The Truro River estuary offers a whole array of water birds, with handy identification guides at Boscawen Park, Trennick Mill pond and Sunny Corner. Curlews are quite common and have a loud, distinctive, mournful call that carries over the water.

what's nearby

The Cathedral dominates the city and was built in the 1880s on the site of a former St Mary's church, which was encompassed into one of the cathedral's aisles. It is well worth a visit. Make sure to view the John Miller painting 'Cornubia, Land of the Saints' on the left, midway down. www.trurocathedral.org.uk

Royal Cornwall Museum – for an insight into many aspects of historic Cornwall.
www.royalcornwallmuseum.org.uk

Enterprise Boats run seasonal boat trips as far as St Mawes and Falmouth, stopping off at Trelissick. There are steps at the quays so beware for those with buggies.
www.falriver.co.uk

other information

TOILETS: There are free public toilets to the south end of Boscawen Park but the disabled toilet needs a RADAR Key (www.radarkeys.org) which if you don't have one can be purchased from the Tourist Information Centre in the middle of Truro.

BUSES: 496 Truro bus station to Malpas –
www.transportforcornwall.co.uk

DOGS: Welcome around Boscawen Park and by the Truro River, they probably wouldn't enjoy the walk through Truro as much.

FREE PARKING: There is free parking at Boscawen Park, there are also charged car parks nearby and the Park and Ride (by Waitrose and the A39/A390) to the east of Truro (TR1 1RH) and at Threemilestone to the west (TR4 9AN) of Truro for cheap wheelchair friendly park and ride for the day - www.cornwall.gov.uk/transport-and-streets/public-transport/cornwalls-transport-services/park-and-ride-services/park-for-truro

FACILITIES

- Boscawen Park has the small 'café in the Park' by the public tennis courts, natural play spaces and playgrounds as well as seasonal bedding and water features.
- On the other side of the road is Trennick Mill Café, adjacent to the pond which is great for ducks and mute swans (please only feed with corn rather than bread).

12

WALK 12

TRURO – IDLESS WOODS
(ST CLEMENT, BISHOP'S, LORD'S AND LADY'S WOODS, TRURO)

FOR A WIDE-PATHED WHEEL IN SOME GORGEOUS MIXED WOODLAND THIS IS JUST THE WALK FOR YOU. IN THIS 131 HECTARE FORESTRY COMMISSION WOODS THERE ARE THREE OPTIONS OF THERE-AND-BACK-AGAIN WALKS (UNFORTUNATELY THE FOOTPATHS THAT POTENTIALLY LINK THE MAIN WHEEL ACCESSIBLE ROUTES ARE A STRUGGLE WITH WHEELS AND ARE TO BE EXPLORED AT MORE ACCESSIBLE TIMES AND/OR WITHOUT WHEELS). THE MAIN ROUTE IS WIDE ENOUGH FOR CHILDREN TO BE ON WHEELS ADJACENT TO A WHEELCHAIR-USER GIVING AN INCLUSIVE GROUP ADVENTURE FEEL.

DISTANCE: Could be up to 4km/2.5 miles if desired.

PARKING: SAT NAV TR4 9QT for Forestry Commission car park or OS Explorer 105 Falmouth and Mevagissey with grid reference 821478. Note: some SAT NAVS will try to take you via Truro crematorium, along a very narrow lane so beware and only go via Truro.

- THE WALK -

Two routes are parallel to small rivers, so as with all walks near water, take care! The other important note is that there are no disabled toilet facilities; the nearest would be in Truro 2km away to the south. The car park/woods are open dawn to dusk.

Variable going for all wheels, good for groups, with compacted hard-core and gravel of different sizes which lends itself mainly to all-terrain wheels. The main path has an incline leading from the car park but provides the best wheels surface of finer compacted gravel.

You need your own transport for this walk as access is via narrow lanes and no public transport is available.

To reach the car park the easiest route is from Truro A39. If driving from the north-east and the St Austell side of Truro, turn right at Trafalgar Roundabout (it has a large Halfords on the corner). Follow the road through two sets of traffic lights, past a large NCP multi storey car park on the left-hand side and then a sharp right-hand bend, straight on at the mini roundabout, underneath the railway bridge and take the second turning to the right with a GR post box set in a stone wall and a sign saying 'Idless 1½' miles.

The road now passes through suburban housing and a primary school is on the right (avoid school arrival and departure times as traffic is grim then). Follow the road for around 500m before taking the turning to the left. This is labelled as a 'quiet lane' and is narrow so drive carefully for about 1.5km where you will find the hamlet of Idless. Once here, bear right on the road and the Forestry Commission car park is 500m further on the right-hand side. Turn right again (Woodman's Café is on the left) and follow the track round - there is ample parking in front of you with more along a turning to the left.

The main walk is at the top of the car park, past the wooden barrier and is in fact a fire break for the woodland. Bear to the left on the main wide gravel track that has a gentle climb up the hill and just keep going for the distance that you feel comfortable with, or to the end which is about 2km in distance and goes past the Iron Age fort after around 1.5km. Once there, enjoy the surroundings before turning back for the return.

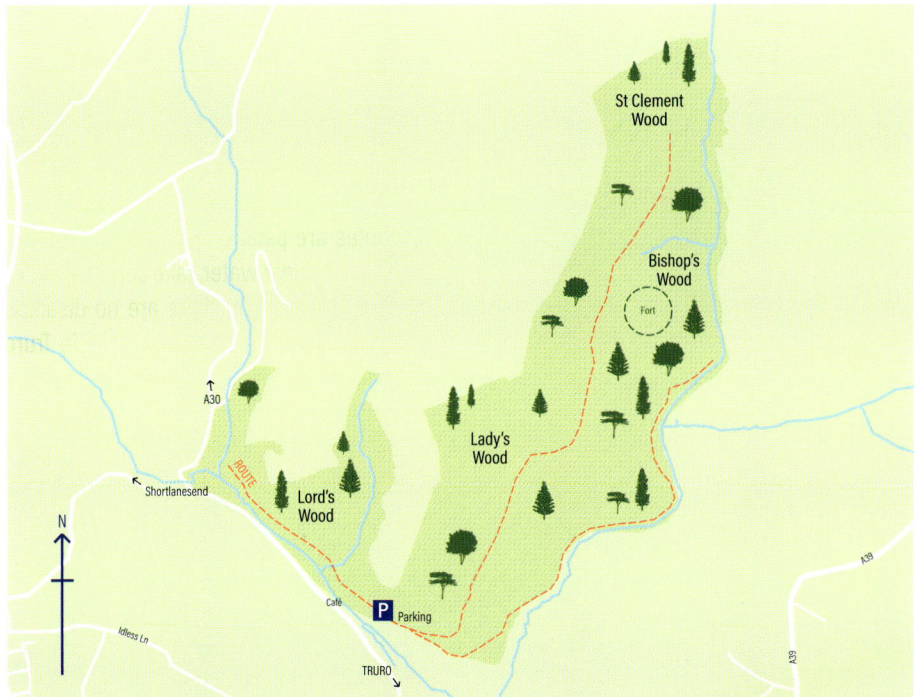

If at the beginning of the main track you bear to the right then the track is gently undulating by the river. This track is a little rougher and better for all-terrain wheels and narrows to a poorer path still after about 750m and is more suitable to those without wheels.

A similar distance path can be taken from the end of the spur of a car park that heads off in a north westerly direction. This is probably the quietest of the three paths. It offers a mini adventure for a non-wheeling adult with children, as at the end of the track it widens out with the track continuing up a steep hill to the right which is too steep for wheels. Walkers could go up this, bear right at the top where there is a pretty narrow path back down to the main track to meet up with the wheeler before the car park.

- WALK EXTENSION -

There are all sorts of paths and tracks that criss-cross the three primary tracks that non-wheelers could do, including walking to Idless from Truro along the lanes.

other information

TOILETS: No disabled toilets, the nearest are in Truro.

BUSES: None available.

DOGS: This is a popular walk for dog walkers, please keep dogs on leads. The Forestry Commission is trying to tackle dog waste with notice boards and disposal facilities by the car park.

OTHER:
- Forestry Commission - www.forestryengland.uk/idless-woods
- Horses - Horse riders need a permit.
- Cyclists and orienteers have the freedom to roam.

FACILITIES

- Car parking is free and quite extensive on a compacted hard-core surface.
- There is a small café adjacent to the car park entrance that gives sustenance to the weary wheeler. It is on the level, mostly open to the elements with a section covered. A basic portable toilet is provided but not for the disabled user.

—NATURE—

The nature here is closely entwined with its history as the protection of one has led to the protection of the other. There is an Iron Age fort with ramparts at the heart of the woods and is noted as a scheduled monument with much evidence of history, such as charcoal making within the ancient oak woodland at its heart. The original 40 acres of wood is noted in the Doomsday Book of 1086; the 13th century saw its conversion into a deer park by the then Bishop of Exeter, giving the top end of the forest 'Bishop's Wood'. Later, the trees started to be felled for tin smelting and tanning and its name changed to Idless.

After WWII the woods became commercialised with larch grown as timber. Now the desire for native species sees the Forestry Commission gradually felling the introduced pines and replanting with more desirable deciduous tree types. This has resulted in Lady's and Lord's woods being ideal locations for children to experience nature first-hand. There is a whole variety of flora, trees, a good range of birds, butterflies and invertebrates which can be regularly and easily spotted. There is a stunning carpet of bluebells in the spring and fungi in the autumn (always beware with fungi unless an expert. I would look, photograph and not touch). Some areas of trees have had shelter building activities going on, so there are plenty of sticks for young ones to occupy themselves in den building.

what's nearby

All that Truro has to offer as Cornwall's County Town!